REVISED EDITION

CORSET CUTTING AND MAKING

First Edition: by W.D.F. Vincent
Second Edition: by Marion McNealy

Acknowledgments

This book would not have been possible without the love and support of many people. First, much thanks goes to my mother for encouraging me to do another kickstarter, even after I'd vowed never to do another one, ever! Thank you to my dear husband, who didn't even question my sanity for deciding to raise the money for this book by running another one, but just sighed and said "Whatever you want to do dear …" and to my son, who kept me company while I worked on the book. Thanks also goes to the amazing team of ladies who contributed to the book: Caroline Woollin, who created the pattern diagrams in CAD from smudgy scans; Nikki Swift, who tested the patterns and made the sample corsets; Liv Free, who modeled and photographed the corsets on a very tight schedule; and Tina Vadász-Hain who designed the book. Thank you to Cathy Hay for her help in promoting the kickstarter and encouragement to tackle this project. Special thanks goes to the trio who oversaw the timing and plans for the whole book: F, S, HS. Thank you for all of your encouragement and strength to complete this project.

My deepest thanks goes to the 250 kickstarter backers, who backed my vision for this book and financially supported this project, this book wouldn't be here without you!

Copyright Statement

Published by Nadel und Faden Press, LLC www.nadelundfadenpress.com

Publisher's Cataloging-in-Publication Data

provided by Five Rainbows Cataloging Services

Names: McNealy, Marion, author. | Vincent, W. D. F. (William D. F.), 1860-1926, author.
Title: Corset cutting and making / Marion McNealy [and] W. D. F Vincent.
Description: Revised and updated edition. | Kennewick, WA : Nadel und Faden Press, 2017. | Previously published in 1924 as "A practical guide to corset cutting and making" by W. D. F. Vincent. | Includes bibliographical references and index.
Identifiers: ISBN 978-0-9985977-1-3 (pbk.)
Subjects: LCSH: Vincent, W. D. F. (William D. F.), 1860-1926. | Corsets--History. | Corsets--Patterns. | Garment cutting. | Foundation garments. | BISAC: DESIGN / Fashion & Accessories.
Classification: LCC TT677 .M392 2017 (print) | DDC 391.4/2--dc23.

ISBN-13: 978-0998597713
ISBN-10: 0998597716
LCCN: 2018930360

Design & Layout: Tina Vadász-Hain, www.expresso-grafik.de
Pattern Diagrams and Flats: Caroline Woollin, www.corsetsbycaroline.co.uk
Sample Corsets constructed and photographed by Nikki Swift, www.narrowedvisions.co.uk
Model, make up, hair and photography: Alivya V Free, www.facebook.com/alivyafreemodel

CONTENTS

PREFACE

When I first started this project, my intention was for it to maintain the historical integrity of the original source, and just re-organize the information and add more to it, to enable the modern reader to better understand the original material. This proved easy to do with the patterns, but as I tackled the introduction and section on corset making, this became much more challenging. The first edition does not appear to be a finished work, as it reads in many places as a set of barely stitched together notes put into a chapter. The information is too much in some places, (tools used for cutting fabric in factories), and too little in others, (the actual methods and process used to make the corsets). I then researched and found other sources from the early 20th century that discussed the methods used in corset factories, which filled in these gaps, but then it became a problem of how to fix a very problematic chapter written by another person. Did I re-write it from scratch? Did I preserve the historical document as an artifact? It began to feel like a doomed group project from grad school where one project member shoddily slapped a few pieces of information together, handed it off to me and went to Disneyland for two weeks without Internet access and didn't return until after the project due date.

So I determined that I would re-write the beginning chapters with a goal of making them usable to the modern corset maker, while preserving key pieces of information, and discarding others which made no sense, and may have been misunderstood by the author of the first edition.The goal of the book after all, was to preserve and pass down knowledge which would be useful to the current field of corsetry, and future readers as well.

To that end, I hope I have been successful, and that this book is as useful to you as I intended it to be.

Marion McNealy
December, 2017

INTRODUCTION

One week in late August 2015, I had an amazing opportunity to view and study many different antique corsets from three different collections: Symington's Collection, Museum of London, and a private collection at the Oxford Conference of Corsetry. After handling so many antiques in such a short period of time, it was quite a shock to feel the heavy physical weight of the modern corsets also on display at the Oxford Conference. The incredible lightness of the antique corsets contrasted with the physical heaviness of the modern corsets made me realize that it was not just the patterning which had been lost in time, but also the construction methods as well. The antique corsets were not heavy in their construction, many being made from one layer of silk, or one layer of thin cotton, and boning of many different materials. They were designed to be worn every day, and many were guaranteed for a year of such wear. The modern corsets, made of many layers of coutil and extensive steel boning, seemed over-engineered for the purpose.

To learn more about the historical construction methods, I began looking for historical information on corset making. One book I happened upon was "A practical guide to corset cutting and making" by W.D.F. Vincent. This rare book is listed in WorldCat as being in only three libraries around the world: The British Library, LACMA, and The State Library of New South Wales, Australia.

The book itself is quite small in size, paper covered and stapled, only 40 pages long. There is no author listed, merely a statement that it is 'By a number of Experts working under the direction and guidance of the Editor of "The Ladies' Tailor" and "Women's Wear Fashions"'. WorldCat lists W.D.F Vincent as the author, presumably as he was the editor of "The Tailor and Cutter", the umbrella publication for those two magazines. W.D.F. Vincent is an understandable suspect, as he was a prolific writer of tailoring books, producing a well known series under the title "The Cutter's Practical Guide to …", with various volumes devoted to women's clothing, boys and girls clothing, men's clothing, shirts and occupational clothing, and an interesting guide to sewing machines.

Exact dating of the book is difficult as there is no copyright statement, or date in the book text, however the British Library copy does have a collection stamp of 25 March, 1924, so it certainly was published by early 1924. The book is in the public domain.

The introduction states:

"The various chapters of this book have in the main been supplied to us by Corset making experts, and we are convinced they will be found comprehensive, and so make the work of great value both to the novice and the experienced Corset maker."

Inside the book, there are 19 corset patterns laid out in the text, as well as two additional patterns for abdominal and supporting belts, and a corset cover, which is very similar to the early type of brassiere.

Where did these patterns come from? This is a hard question to answer, as there is no actual source listed, or referenced, beyond the nebulous "experts", however, a few potential sources are the English magazines "The Ladies' Tailor" and "Women's Wear Fashions", both of which W.D.F. Vincent edited, or French fashion and lingerie magazines, such as La Mode Illustree and Les Dessous Élégants. Both of these magazines are known to have published corset patterns. Although neither of them have large collections of digitized editions, a few editions of Les Dessous Élégants are available online at Wikimedia Commons. The January 1914 edition of Les Dessous Élégants boasts that the magazine will contain 9 corset patterns and 3 lingerie patterns throughout the year. The January issue included the first pattern, which sadly is not online, although the illustration and instructions are available.[1] Les Dessous Élégants was aimed at an international audience, as the instructions for the corset pattern are in French, English, German, Spanish and Italian.

Perhaps there was an unknown corset pattern designer who provided the patterns, or maybe a company provided them? Advertised in the American publication "The Corset and Underwear Review" is a possible pattern source which most certainly had British counterparts:

Learn Corset Designing
Pattern Grading
Four weeks course personal instruction teaches you how
Evening classes for men – Cutters Get ready for Fall positions
Our system fits you for big wholesale positions as Designers.
Write Today
Special Course By Mail on Corset making and Designing fits you for business for yourself.
Pattern and materials complete, $15.00.
The Greenwood School of Corset Designing

500 Fifth Avenue, New York
Corset and Underwear Review, July 1921[2]

Whatever the source, of these patterns, the patterns range date from 1900 to 1920, and are placed in the book in no specific order. Although the introduction of the first edition states:

"We have deemed it desirable to include a selection of Diagrams illustrative of the older styles as well as the modern types, for they illustrate a variety of principles which cannot fail to be suggestive to the designer, and it is quite impossible to say how soon fashions may change, and the older styles may once again find favour."

This mix of different decades of corsets strikes one as odd, because there is no attempt to explain or illustrate the cutting principles of the different styles, just the patterns and a few words on the materials and construction methods needed for each corset. Indeed, the first edition seems to have been a project which was started well before World War 1, put aside during the war, and then hurriedly finished to get it published after W.D.F Vincent retired in 1921.[3] The oldest corset styles are at the back of the book, and the newest styles at the front, with lingerie fashion plates for 1922-23 included at the beginning. The first edition appears to be created from a stack of notes, taken out of a drawer, and put together, most recent at the beginning to oldest at the end, to create the book.

While the exact story behind the original order of the content has been hidden by the passing of the decades, I have taken the liberty of dating, naming and re-organizing all the patterns, and liberally adding information where I think it is required, to create this second edition. Quotes from the first edition are formated in **italics,** quotes from other sources and new research gathered for this book, are presented in regular font. Hopefully this new edition will enable the modern reader to use and explore the unique styles contained in the book, and inspire others in the future.

MATERIALS

The materials which were used in corset making vary widely based on geographic location, and decade. Different materials fell in and out of fashion, and were also affected by world events and market pressures. A survey of mail order catalogs from the United States and Canada from 1900 to 1922 reveals some interesting trends in corset materials and colors. Although mail order catalogs will obviously not give a full picture of all available consumer options, as there were custom corset makers and high-end corset lines which had access to different materials and colors.

From 1900 to 1908, the most commonly available corset colors were white, black or drab, and they came in a wide variety of materials. Coutil was the most widely available corset fabric.

The 1902 Chas A Stevens catalog lists corsets in the following materials and colors:
· Coutil, white or drab
· Sateen, black, white or drab
· Batiste, white, pink or blue
· Dainty flowered silk
· Roman cloth, black or white
· Italian cloth, black
· Silk brocade, with cream ground flowered in pink or lavender.

And one extremely expensive corset (2127) came in the following fabrics:
· Silk corset rep in white, pink, blue and black
· Light grey silk, flowered with pink rosebuds
· Blue and gold brocade

As the decade progressed, the fabric choices and the number of colors decreased.
1905-1906 Fall Winter Macy's Catalog
· Coutil, white or drab
· Satin, black
· Sateen, black
· Batiste, white
· Fancy broche in white, pink and white, white and blue, or black
· Linen, white

By 1908, the catalogs change to just offering white coutil, white batiste, or white jean as possible options. There are still a few special corsets, mainly nursing corsets, available in drab. Over the next few years, even drab is dropped from the list of colors available, and some catalogs don't even bother to continue to list the color, just the fabric, since white was the only color option.

This continues until 1915, when pink becomes an option for high-end corsets. In January 1916, Warner Brothers begins advertising a line of Debutante corsets in brocade, batiste and coutil, in both white and pink.[4] Although pink does not appear in the mail-order catalog listings until the Fall of 1917, and then only in a few, the customers were buying pink corsets from retail stores.

In August 1917, the Canadian Dry Goods Review reports "New York is beginning to call white corsets "old-fashioned" so strongly are buyers taking up the pink lines."[5]

The "Conditions in the Corset Field" report for Fall 1917 states:
"The coutil models are selling best, with broches holding up well, but batistes are not so good. Pink, leads in the matter of colors, about ten pink corsets selling to one white. Practically no other color has assumed any prominence, although some orchid models have been featured and have sold quite well, and also a scattering of blue. There is a marked difference, for instance, between the demand that exists in this country and that which exists in South America. There the favorite colors are amber, blue, orchid, the palest of greens, and also some pink. An up-to-date window display in a high class corset shop in one of the South American capitals is almost kaleidoscopic in its bewildering color effects."

However, not all customers were convinced that a pink corset was a good idea, even if it was fashionable, the report also commented:
"In the smaller towns throughout New England and the Middle West, as in the South, white corsets still lead. This is probably due to a sense of thriftiness, as a great many women are not yet convinced that colored and fancy corset materials wear fully as well as the plain white coutils."

The Corset and Underwear Review. v. 10 October 1917[6]

Although pink was now available alongside of white, those would be the only colors available to the catalog buyer through the end of the Teens and into the Twenties, and by the end of the Twenties, pink would be the main color option, with only a few corsets being offered in white

1918-1919 Perry Dame Catalog
· Coutil, white
· Silk-finish Brocade, White or Flesh Pink
· Mercerized Brocade, Flesh, Pink or White

1919 Bellas Hess Catalog
· Coutil, white
· Mercerized Brocade, white or flesh-pink

1920-21 Eatons Catalog
· Coutil, white
· Coutil, pink
· Cotton brocade, pink

1922 Charles Williams Catalog
· Coutil, pink
· Coutil, white
· Brocade, flesh colored

BONING
During the period 1900-1922 there were several boning options available: whalebone, or an imitation; steel boning; and later, spiral boning.

Bones
In the early 1900s, whalebone was still commonly available, and used in high-end corsets. By 1909 however, the whaling fleet was in decline, due to a limited number of whaling ships, smaller number of whales and much lower prices for whalebone, because of the many substitutes[7] available. The imitation whalebones, such as "Ariston Boning" and "Wahlon", were advertised as being rustless, without odor, and much cheaper to use than whalebone. However, corsets fully boned with whalebone were still being advertised in August 1909.[8] But by 1913, the Spirella catalog commented on how impossible whalebone was to obtain for corsets,[9] and recommends ladies switch to corsets boned with their flexible wire bones.

HELENE
SAVOY SATIN IN CELESTIAL BLUE, BY JAMES HARE
LACE FROM LACETIME ON ETSY
CORSET CONSTRUCTED BY NIKKI SWIFT, NARROWED VISIONS CORSETS
PHOTOGRAPHY BY NIKKI SWIFT

Steels

Although most catalog listings do not list the boning material, when they do, the most common one is steel. Often the listings simply state "steel filled", but when more information is included, they usually advertise the flexibility and unbreakable qualities of the boning:

"Boned throughout with finest tempered capped end steels, with ten extra quality side steels, making this corset absolutely unbreakable."[10]

"Boned throughout with extra strong pliant steels absolutely rust proof."[11]

Spirals – Wire Boning

Spirella Corset company was founded, and began making corsets, in 1904 with it's patented flexible wire bones. This 1912 demonstration example of their spiral bone shows how simple a design it was. In 1914, they patented two new shapes of wire bone, neither of which look like today's spiral bones at all. There were several other types in use as well, such as this looped wire boning from 1918.

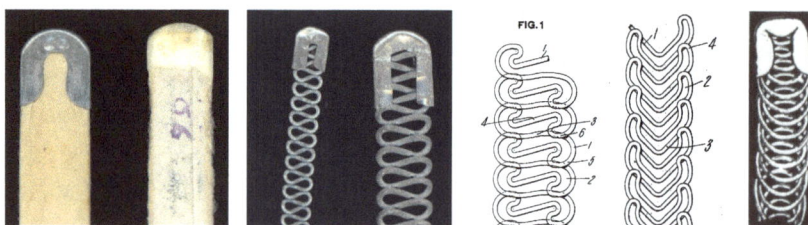

Types of Steel and Wire Boning
Left to right:
Paper covered steel bones, 1912 Spirella spiral bones, 1914 Spirella patent US1193790 bone, 1914 Spirella patent US1193742 bone, Looped wire boning from 1918 catalog listing.[12]

The earlier patterns in the book make a distinction where steels and bones should be used, to provide different levels of flexibility in the finished corset. When the word "bone" is marked in the pattern diagrams, it indicates that the maker should use either whalebone, or a whalebone substitute in that place. When "steel" is marked on the pattern diagram, this indicates that the maker should use flat steel bones, and in the case of "side steel" the bone should be a wide steel bone.

The later patterns do not mark the boning channels, or the type of boning to be used on the patterns, because the bones mainly followed the seam lines and the choice was limited to either spiral steel or flat steel.

BUSKS

Several different types of busks were commonly available, as seen in this listing of busk options from the 1920 Spirella Catalog.

Straight Busk – in two widths; 1/2 inch for back-laced corsets, and 3/8 inch wide for front laced corsets. Twenty-four lengths, 8 1/2 to 20 inches. Made of the best clock spring steel.

Tapering Busk – 1 inch wide at bottom, tapering to 3/8 inch wide at top. Twenty-three lengths, 9 to 20 inches. Made of high grade steel.

Spoon Busk – 3/8 wide at top, 1 1/8 inch at widest part near bottom. Seventeen lengths, 10 to 18 inches. Curves inward at bottom. Made of high grade steel.

Flexible Busk – 1/2 wide. Eleven lengths, 9 to 14 inches. Covered with white rubberized cloth. Soft and pliable.

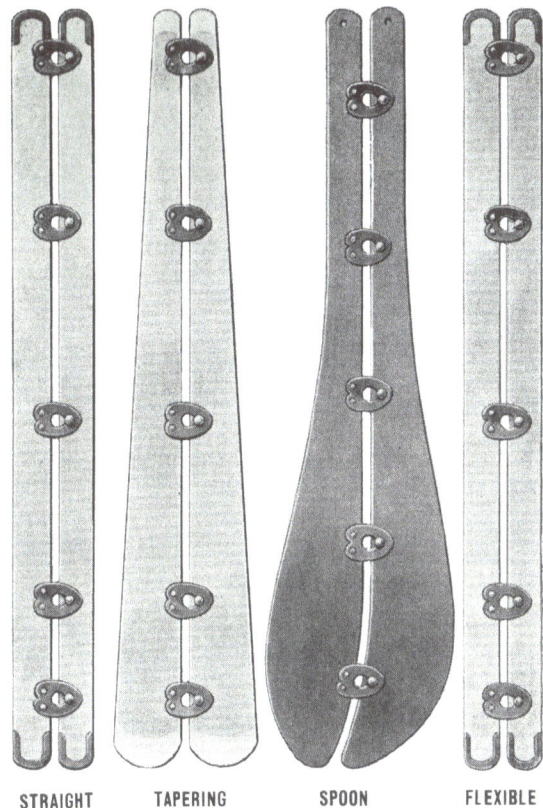

STRAIGHT   TAPERING   SPOON   FLEXIBLE

All busks are graduated in half-inch lengths, and have heavy triple-plated, nickeled hooks. Busks under 10 inches, four hooks; from 10 to 15 inches, five hooks; above 15 inches, six hooks.

CONSTRUCTION

The first edition of Corset Cutting and Making has a small amount of general information on the construction processes, which matches the methods used on corsets in the late 1910s to early 1920s. While some of the patterns do include detailed construction information, including order of sewing operations, or the type of seams to be used, other patterns have no information.

For a more complete understanding of corset construction methods, two useful US Government reports from 1913 and 1914, on processes and working conditions in the corset industry have been combined with the information from the first edition to create an overview of the construction process.

CUTTING

The first step described by all sources is the cutting out of the corset exterior fabric, along with all internal linings, strappings, and interlinings.

Exterior Fabric

"The procedure for marking out corsets, whether a single pair or in quantities, is much the same. Spread the cloth on to the bench, [with the] grain, or pattern, underneath, so that all markings are made on the wrong side of the material, and will consequently be covered by the strapping."

Linings

"Front and back linings from drill or coutil, according to the quality of the corsets, are next cut. For lining the fronts (busks) cut the strips 1 1/2 inches wide, and slightly longer than front pattern. For wedge, or spoon busks, wider at the bottom and narrow at the top. Back linings are cut 1 3/4 inches wide"

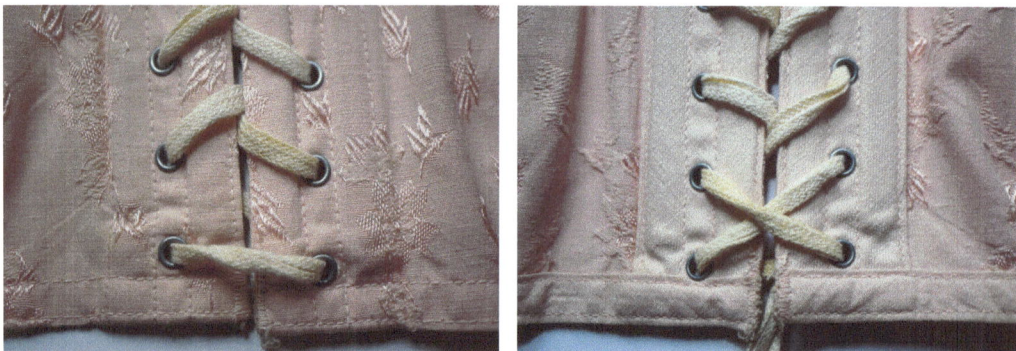

CLOSE UP OF THE EXTERIOR AND INTERIOR LINING OF THE BACK LACES OF A MID-1920'S CORSET.
PRIVATE COLLECTION

Facings

Beginning in the mid-1910s, an external facing was used for the busk, along with a lining, for some styles of corsets, especially those with elastic sections at the top or bottom at the front of the corset. This was a separate piece, usually straight, cut from the outer fabric, and is not shown on the pattern diagrams. Only the Vivian pattern, p.100, mentions specifically that there is to be a facing, and that is not included in the pattern diagram. However, the original illustrations for Ruby, p.90, and Myrtle, p.96, also show an external facing, which appears to be applied on top of the front pattern pieces, and is not an additional section added to the corset.

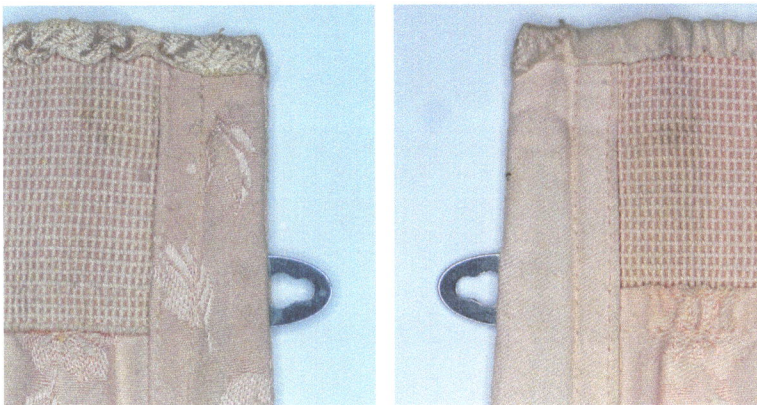

CLOSE UP OF THE EXTERIOR FACING AND INTERIOR LINING OF THE FRONT BUSK OF A MID-1920'S CORSET. THIS IS IS INTERLINED WITH A DOUBLE LAYER OF COTTON FABRIC. PRIVATE COLLECTION

Interlinings

The interlinings are a protective layer between the boning materials and the outer fabric, helping to cushion the ends of the bones to prevent wear-through. The interlining for the bone channels is folded in half, and tucked inside the bone channel before it is sewn down.

The busk covers, or busk wrap, helps to soften the sharp edges of the metal, protecting the front edge stitching from ripping out.

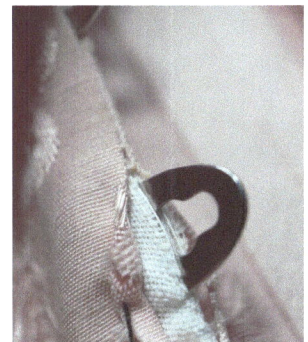

CLOSE UP OF THE DOUBLE LAYER OF FOLDED INTERLINING FABRIC WHICH COVERS THE BUSK IN A MID-1920'S CORSET. PRIVATE COLLECTION

"The interlinings come next. Take Wigan, or other suitable material. Busk covers are cut to suit the width of the busks, 1 1/2 inches being the general width for straight busks, and 2 1/2 inches for wedge, shaped to fit into outer linings. Interlining for strapping is cut 3/4 inch wide for two-bone and side-steel, but the width is necessarily governed by that of the steels to be used."

Wigan is a woven cotton interlining still used in tailoring today.

Strapping

The bone or steel strappings, known now as bone channels or casings, were cut from drill, a lightweight twill. For seam strappings, a tightly woven cotton, similar to a quilting cotton broadcloth, was often used.

"Cut bone or side steel (strapping) according to the width of steels, and whether one or two bone strappings are required. For side steels and two-bone strapping, the usual width is 1 1/4 inches, and for single back steels 1 inch. The strapping is usually cut in 12-yard lengths to prevent undue waste in short ends."

CLOSE UP OF A SEAM, SEWN AS A PLAIN SEAM, AND THEN COVERED WITH A DOUBLE BONE CASING ON THE INSIDE. NOTICE THAT THE CENTER LINE OF THE BONE CASING IS NOT DIRECTLY ON THE SEAM, BUT OFF CENTER, SECURING THE SEAM ALLOWANCE AND CREATING A SINGLE WELT SEAM. THE BONE CASING IS INTERLINED WITH A DOUBLE LAYER OF COTTON FABRIC, SIMILAR TO THE BUSK. MID-1920'S CORSET. PRIVATE COLLECTION

ORDER OF CONSTRUCTION

The first step differs between the accounts. The 1913 report states that the gores should be put in first, the 1914 report says that first the main seams are sewn, and then the gores are put in. The correct order of operation would of course depend on the type of corset being constructed.

Folding

"The first operation on the corset after it is taken from the cutters to the women operatives is folding. This simple process is the preliminary preparation for certain seams. The pieces are fed into a machine which turns over a narrow fold of the cloth and presses it firmly down, so that when the pieces go to the stitcher this fold can be stitched down flat, making what is called a lap seam. In many factories folding is not done as a separate operation, but the same machine that stitches the seam folds the cloth as it is fed in. In the case of heavy material folding is necessary."[13]

Gore Making

"After the pieces have been cut, out the edges of the gores are folded down by hand, a simple operation, usually performed by young girls who have recently come into the factory, after which they go to the gore maker. Her work is to put the gore into the main body pieces of the corset. Owing to the triangular shape of the gore this is one of the most difficult of the operations on a corset. The gore maker has to sew up into the corner of the gore and around it, so that her seam forms an acute angle. Because of this fact she can use only a single needle machine, and therefore has to sew two seams on each gore to correspond to the lap seam with which the rest of the pieces are joined. Most of the gores have to be put in with a curved instead of a straight seam, so that the gore maker must pay close attention to the feed of the goods through the machine. Any carelessness on her part may result in spoiling the corsets, as their shape depends very largely upon her work."[14]

Joining, Seaming or Closing

"The pieces go next to the girls who do the stitching known variously as assembling, seaming, joining or closing. This operation joins together the pieces which are to form the complete garment. The pieces are stitched together either with a plain seam, by a one-needle machine (the edges being left unfinished and covered later by stripping), or with a lap seam, where the edges are turned under and stitched down by a two-needle machine. This operation is known as lap-seam felling. The plain seaming is the simplest machine stitching there is. Where the pieces to be joined together are cut on the bias, or crossways of the cloth, the operation is called bias seaming, and is more difficult on account of the tendency of the bias edge to stretch and get out of shape unless skillfully handled."[15]

Putting on Belts

"The tape which forms the waistband inside the corset is pasted on by hand or by machine, or is tacked or basted by the flossing machine. Either of these operations is known as "belts". The basting stitches are pulled out of the belt after the strips and steels are stitched across it, as these are enough to keep it in place."[16]

Steel Stitching

"From the lap seamer the work goes to the skip stitcher, who seams down the outside edge of the coverings or lacings for the front steels (busks). This is done on a single-needle machine and has no special points of difficulty or interest. Next the stripper puts on the strips which make the pockets into which the bones or steels are slipped. This is done on two, three, or four needle machines, according to the style of the corset and whether the operator is doing side, back, or body stripping. The two steels used in the front of the corsets are slipped into the cover made by the skip stitcher and the work is ready for the steel stitcher.

Steel stitching consists of stitching the front steels (busks) into the facings by running a single seam down the inner edge of the busk, as close to it as possible. This is one of the hardest of the machine operations, owing to the necessity of holding the front steels (busks) as close to the needle as can, be done. The work is done on a single-needle machine"[17]

Stripping

"The narrow, flexible steels (or "wires") which are used in pairs or in threes at the sides of the corset can be stitched in like the front and side steels, but are sometimes pushed in by hand. Stripping is the process of stitching "strip" or facing to the under side of the corset to case these wires. There are two kinds of strip, – either a finished tape is used or strips of material cut out and folded along both edges by machine and wound into large rolls (winding stripping). The operatives by using multiple needle machines make three or four rows of stitching at once, according to the number of wires to be inserted, – three rows for two wires, four rows for three wires. The more needles the machine has the greater the skill required, and piece rates for stripping vary accordingly."[18]

Back-stitching

"The back of a corset usually has a pair of wires at each side, which are inserted, like the side wires, by the boners (see "boning"), after back strips have been stitched on with a four-needle machine. Back-stitching is the process of stitching on these back strips, which differs from ordinary stripping in that the raw edge of the corset has to be turned in under the strip. Individual styles of corset, however, vary from this general practice."[19]

Boning

"The corsets next go to the boners, – young girls who push the wires (or "bones") under the casing strips by hand. They use a small wooden tool like a crochet hook to open the end of the casing and work with remarkable speed, inserting two or three bones at a time, but the work requires little skill. From these beginners the forewomen, who are watching for signs of ability, select girls to learn the more difficult operations. Although this process is still called boning, very little whalebone is now used in ready-made corsets, the "bones" being strips of flexible steel. In many factories the wires are put in at the same time the cloth strips are put on and therefore no boners are employed."[20]

Barring or Flossing

"When the bones have been pushed into their cases the open ends are closed with a short row or "bar" of stitching. On the more expensive corsets these ends after being barred are stayed or reinforced by satin stitching across them with the flossing machine. Sometimes both these operations are called flossing."[21]

Shaping

"At this stage the corsets, made up as far as the body is concerned, are sent to the shaper, who trims off the upper and lower edges, making the curves regular and shaping them to conform to the desired style. Two methods of shaping were seen in use, in one the work being done by hand with a pair of scissors, while in the other it is done by machine."[22]

Binding

"The shaped top and bottom edges are next bound with a strip of braid or other folded material, using one or two rows of stitching. Sometimes a draw string is put in the upper edge, and hose supporters on the lower edge, in the process of binding."[23]

CLOSE UP OF THE EXTERIOR AND INTERIOR OF THE UPPER EDGE BINDING, AND LOWER EDGE BINDING OF A MID-1920'S CORSET. PRIVATE COLLECTION

Cutting Ends, End-stitching and Finishing

"The unfinished ends of binding and loose ends of thread left by the stitchers are next cut off, and in the better grade of corsets the raw edges of binding are finished at the end by hand or machine stitching."[24]

Eyeletting and Hook-punching

"These are the two processes for which a punch machine is used. The eyeletting machine punches the rows of holes for corset laces. The corset is then fed along automatically under two punches, the first of which cuts out circular holes in the cloth into which the second inserts metal rims or eyelets, folds them over and presses them down tightly. The hook-punch punches in the hook and eye which fasten the corset below the front steels."[25]

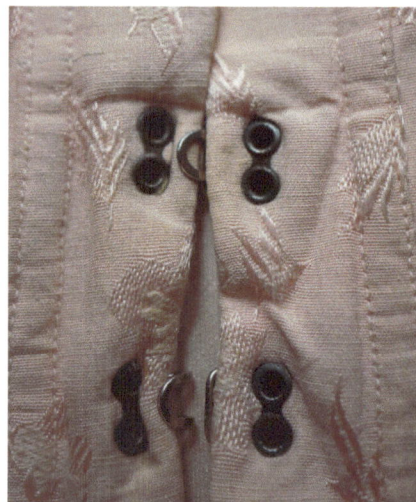

CLOSE UP OF THE HOOKS AND EYES UNDER THE BUSK, FROM A MID-1920'S CORSET. PRIVATE COLLECTION

Top Trimming, Lace Stitching, Lace Tacking and Flossing

"The tops of corsets are variously ornamented. Usually lace or embroidery (known as Hamburg) is used. The trimming is first stitched along the top edge of the corset, and its lower edge is then tacked down at intervals between the steels with the flossing machine or (in high-grade corsets) by hand. Sometimes top trimming and binding are done at the same time, or (in the cheapest corsets) top trimming takes the place of top binding"[26]

Ironing

"Some styles of corsets are starched before ironing, and some are merely dampened, each ironer doing that part of the work on his own lot of corsets. A special room is used for dampening or starching the corsets, which is done by means of a fine spray of starch vapor or steam. When the ironer has dampened or starched a batch of corsets, he carries them back to his ironing bench, on which is placed a small raised ironing board or pad. The special point to be observed in the ironing is to keep the gores from getting creased. To avoid this, when the gores are ironed the iron must be managed with one hand while the corset must be pulled or stretched out with the other, and at the same time the weight of the body must be thrown onto the iron to give the necessary pressing. In the factories visited the irons did not swing on brackets, but had to be lifted to and from the corsets; they weighed from 10 to 12 pounds"[27]

Matching, Numbering, Measuring and Stamping

"The finished corsets are next measured, matched and stamped with their size number and style number or name. Sometimes a label with the name of the style has already been stitched in by the binder, stripper or hand-sewer."[28]

Second Examining, Final Examining or Inspecting.

"The corsets are finally inspected for imperfections, and when these have been remedied they are ready for shipping."[29]

LILLIE
SAVOY SATIN IN ENGLISH ROSE, BY JAMES HARE
LACE FROM LACETIME ON ETSY
CORSET CONSTRUCTED BY NIKKI SWIFT, NARROWED VISIONS CORSETS
PHOTOGRAPHY BY NIKKI SWIFT

THE PATTERNS

The patterns have been redrawn from the originals, and tested to ensure a functioning pattern. The original drafting format, seen below, has been preserved, and an alternative view of the pattern on a standard grid format has also been prepared. On the opposite page, is a table of the finished corset measurements, and their recommended construction.

How to draft the pattern

1) Using an inch ruler, begin by marking a 0 and drawing a vertical line, and a horizontal line from that point.

2) On the vertical line, measure down from the 0 and mark the the various starting points for the horizontal lines as seen on the diagram, for instance 1, 3 3/4, 18

3) From those marks, draw out 90 degree horizontal lines, these will become the bust or top edge, waist, hip and/or lower edge lines.

4) On the top line, the 0 line, mark out the top edge points, and continue for the bust, waist, hip and/or lower edge lines.

5) Connect the dots with smooth curves to finish the pattern.

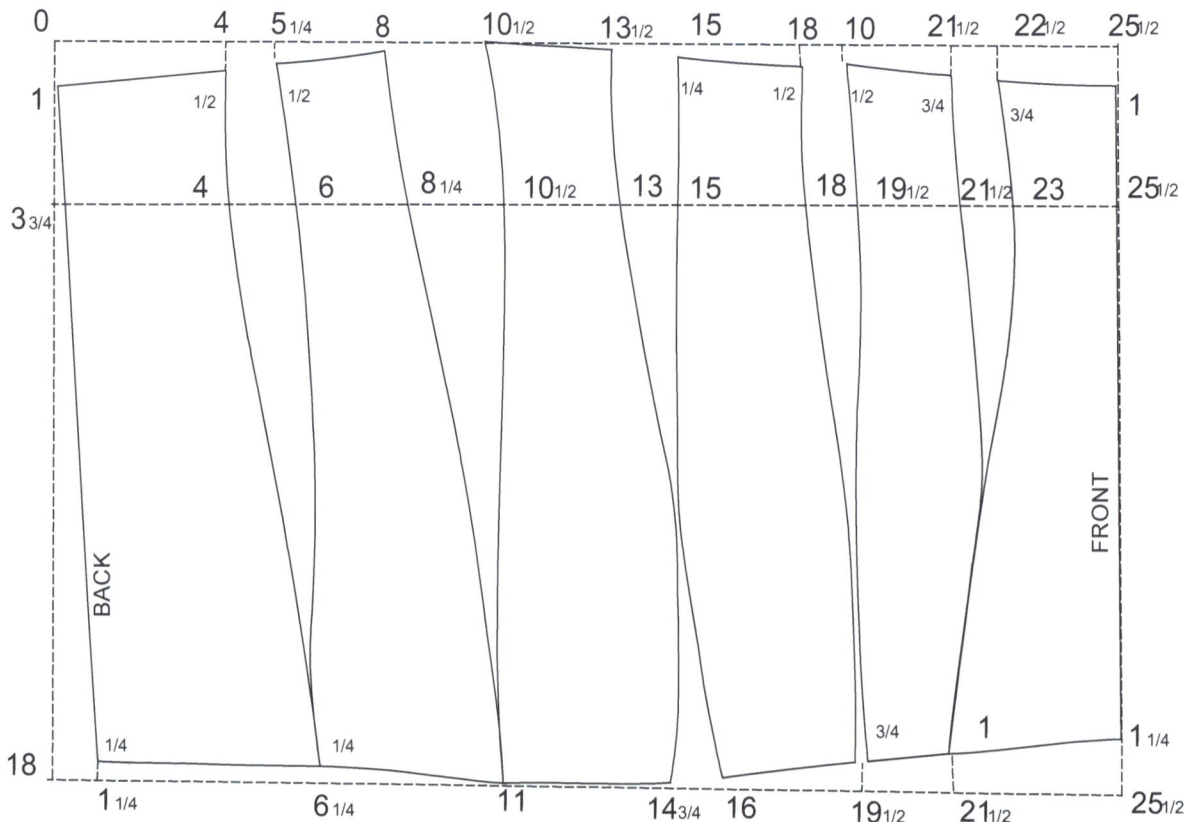

| Name | Date | Pattern Measurements in Inches | | | Recommended Construction | | |
		Bust or Top	Waist	Hip	Seam Type	Boning Channels	Boning
Serafina	1900-1905	35	25	37	Double welted	External	Imitation Whalebone and Steel
Elsie	1902	40	24	42	Double welted	Internal	Imitation Whalebone and Steel
Lillie	1902	36	22	40	Double welted	Internal	Imitation Whalebone and Steel
Lorna	1902	36	21	33	Plain seam, covered with boning channel	External	Imitation Whalebone and Steel
Isobel	1900-1904	37	25	38	Double welted	Internal	Imitation Whalebone
Helene	1905-1906	36	22	38	Plain seam, covered with internal strip	Internal	Imitation Whalebone and Steel
Olive	1904-1908	37	22	33	Double welted	Internal	Imitation Whalebone and Steel
Madeline	1902-1908	36	23	34	Double welted	Internal	Imitation Whalebone and Steel
Millie	1907	39	25	37	Double welted	Internal	Imitation Whalebone and Steel
Thelma	1911-1912	34	31	36	Plain seam, covered with boning channel	Internal	Steel
Corset Cover-Brassiere	1905-1913	40	24		Plain seam, covered with boning channel	Internal	Imitation Whalebone
Mary	1914-1918	31	28	34	Plain seam, covered with boning channel	Internal	Imitation Whalebone
Lillian	1916-1918	39	28	33	Plain seam, covered with boning channel	Internal	Steel and or Spirals
Clara	1916-1920	36	35	40	Plain seam, covered with boning channel	Internal	Steel and or Spirals
Ruby	1917-1921	36	31	43	Plain seam, covered with boning channel	Internal	Steel and or Spirals
Myrtle	1918	39	34	39	Plain seam, covered with boning channel, and Double Welted	Internal	Steel and or Spirals
Vivian	1919-1921	27	24	30	Plain seam, covered with boning channel	Internal	Steel and or Spirals

SERAFINA

HORIZONTAL SEAMED CORSET 1900-1905

The next style of corset to be considered is one especially suitable for those figures who desire to be tight-laced. The seams of the various gores are cleverly constructed, so as to run horizontally round the figure, and may terminate at any height when properly put together, provide for much more strain in that direction.

Coutil is certainly the most suitable material, or any other may be used, as desired. We illustrate on our diagram on the next page , the smallest number of bones and steels it is advisable to use, and where the number is required to be added to, they may be located as follows: Bones will be arranged to cover the small vees between steels and other sets of bones.

When cutting out, take care to place the eyelet edge on the straight of material; also that the top and bottom edges are cut 1/2 inch wider than pattern on each band, so that each edge may be overlapped, have its inlay turned in, and then the seams may be stitched in ordinary tailor fashion on either side.

ON PREVIOUS PAGE SERAFINA
SAVOY SATIN IN MAURITIUS, BY JAMES HARE
LACE FROM LACETIME ON ETSY
CORSET CONSTRUCTED BY NIKKI SWIFT, NARROWED VISIONS CORSETS
MODEL, MAKE UP, HAIR AND PHOTOGRAPHY: ALIVYA V FREE

The dot and dash line shows the waist hollow, and when cutting the vees thereon, crease the parts, then sew before slitting the edges of same with a penknife; or if the material is very thin, then a little stretching of the creased edges will suffice for the cutting, after which they may be neatly felled or stitched down.

These corsets are cut in ten parts: the half, as shown here, has three upper and two lower portions.

Corsets are made from two broad bands of elastic joined together in this style for athletic purposes.

Corsets with seams placed on the horizontal or diagonal, instead of the vertical, are not unknown throughout the history of corset design, but they are not in the majority of surviving examples. This particular corset is the last pattern listed in the first edition, although it is probably one of the earliest patterns, dating to 1900-1905.

This early date based on two pieces of evidence. In the 1904 General Price List of Jeremiah Rotherman & Co (London, England), listed amoung the many different corsets available for sale, is one called the "Horozone", with five horizontal bands,[30] just as this pattern has. It is listed as a black corset, soft finished, with a 13 1/2" straight busk, for quality A corsets, fanned (flossed) with gold, price was 47/6, and for quality D, fanned with coral, 78/-.

There is no brand name associated in the catalog with this "Horozone" corset. However in a 1906 United Kingdom patent design suit, the Charles Bayer company is listed as selling a corset with the same name in 1900, 1902 and 1904, and advertised it in 1905.[31] Although the placement of the bones in the pattern and the illustration are not the same, in the legal proceedings, the Charles Bayer company is noted for changing their boning layout on their corsets from season to season.

HOROZONE.

HOROZONE CORSET
1904 GENERAL PRICE LIST OF
JEREMIAH ROTHERMAN & CO (UK)

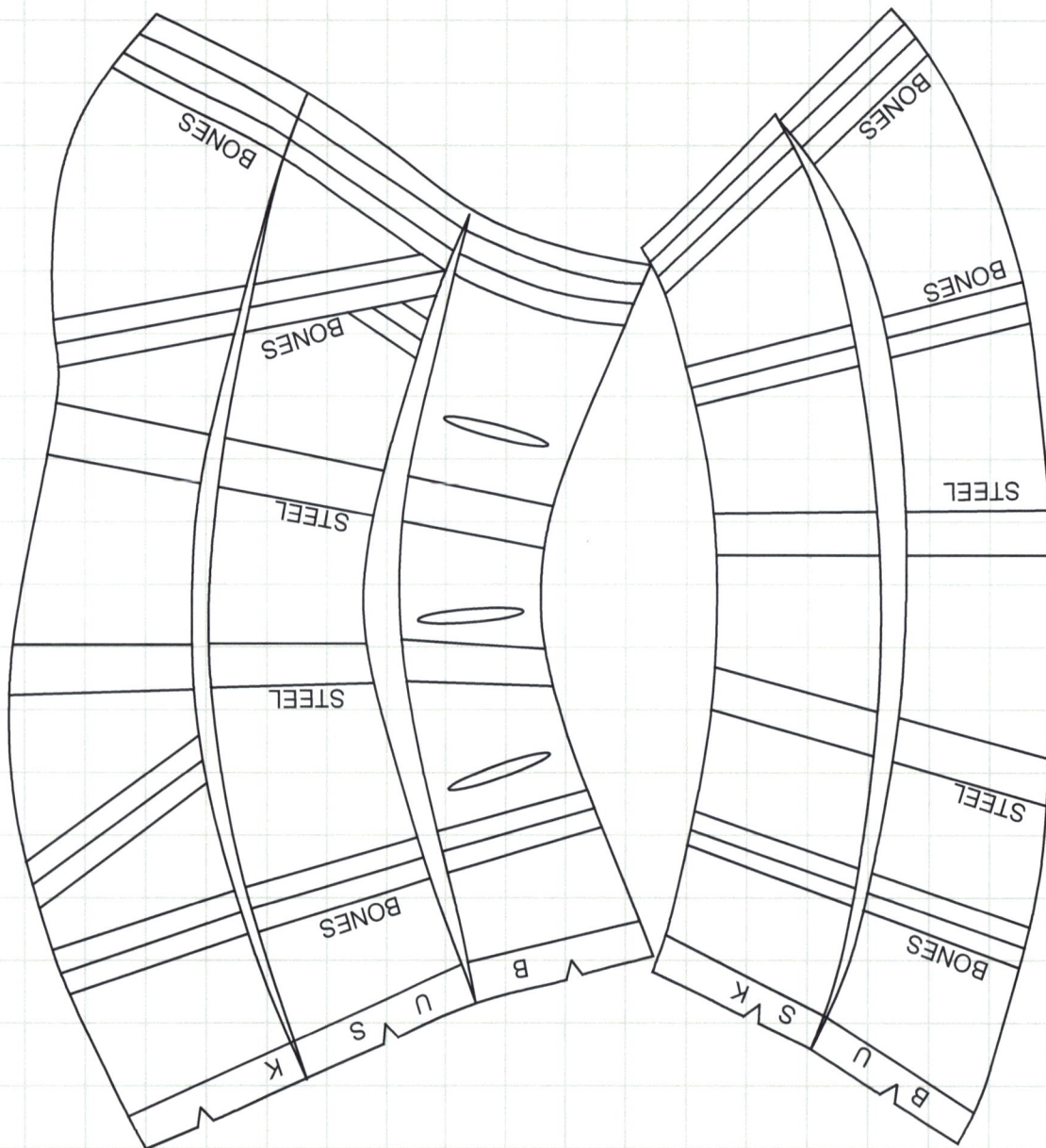

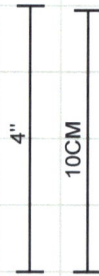

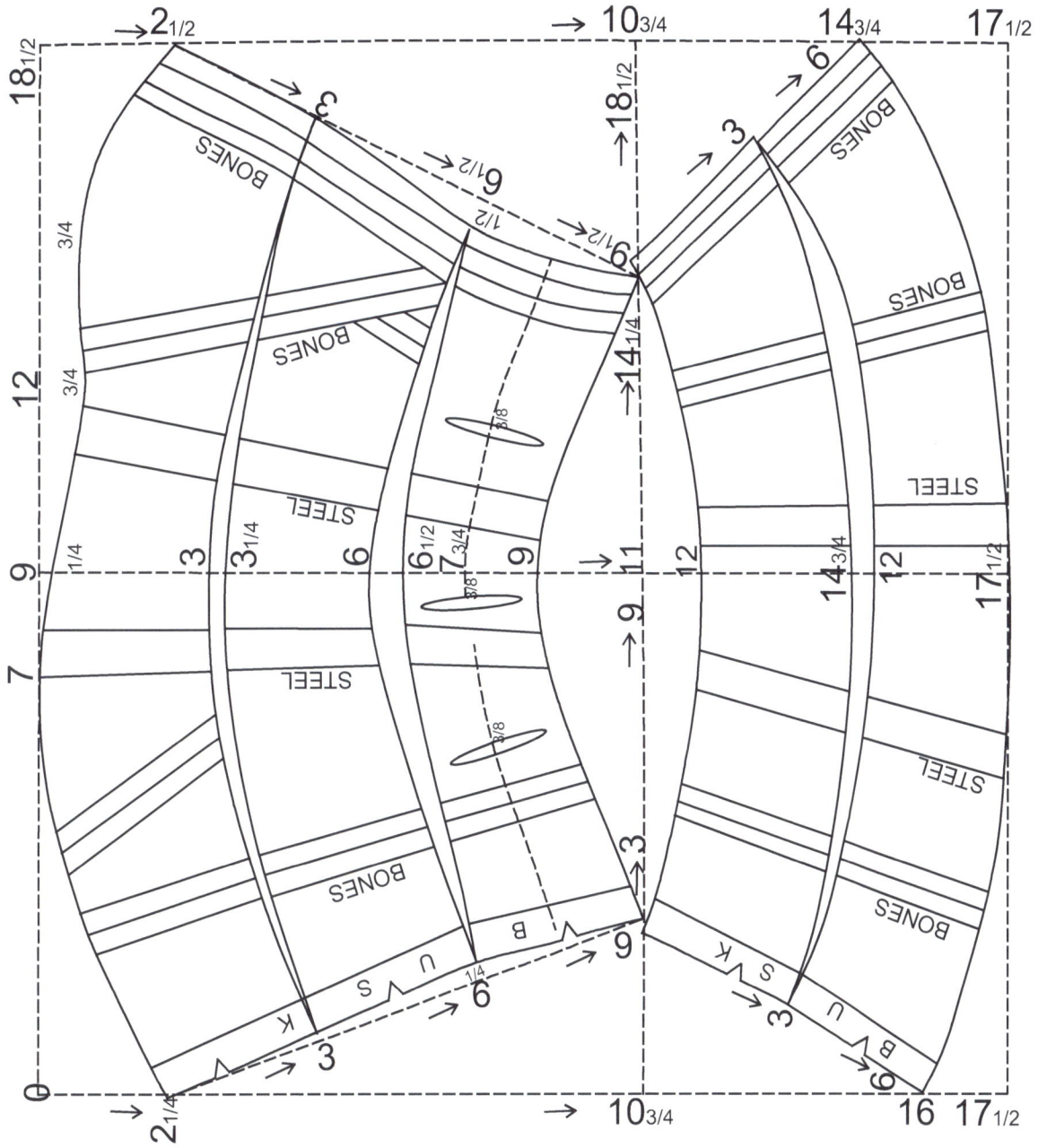

Elsie

Straight front corset 1902

This style of corset will, if well made, transform the shape of the stout figure, imparting to it a lady-like, stylish and fashionable contour. It is cut on a principle which will compress the lower part of the figure in front below the waist without undue pressure, whilst at the same time it allows plenty of spring over the hips and seat, admitting an easy gait to the most squatty figure. For ladies who suffer from internal disorders this corset will be found a great support. On the accompanying diagram we are showing how to cut a flat-fronted corset for a stout figure. The measures to which the diagram is drafted are, 40 chest, 24 waist, and 42 hips.

As will be seen, the bodypart is cut in two parts, there being two gussets for the breasts and four gussets over the hips and seat; each of these is marked, respectfully, A, B, C, D, E, and F. These must be inserted at the places marked. In order to make this quite clear, we have indicated corresponding notches, so that there can be no difficulty in putting it together.

In cutting from the material, place the straight sides of all the pieces on the top edge, or parallel with the selvedge of the material.

Tape and bone according to instructions given on previous pages, and trim the top with ribbon and lace, according to taste.

This corset is similar in design to two corsets in the 1902 Chas A Stevens catalog, both of which are also for full, or stout, figures. The designation of "stout" here, does not refer to the waist size of 24 inches, but the larger bust and hip measurement, 40 in. chest and 42 in. hips than the standard measurements of 35 in. chest and 41 in. hip.[32]

While these particular catalog listings do not mention it, many corsets of this style, in this year, were advertised as being bias gored. The pattern instructions seem to suggest this, but are not entirely clear on this particular point, however a 1899 corset pattern from La Mode Pratique instructs that the gores are to be cut on the bias.
Cutting the panel and gores on the bias would allow for them to smoothly stretch over the bust and hips, resulting in a comfortable corset. The bust is low cut, allowing for support, but not compression of the bust.

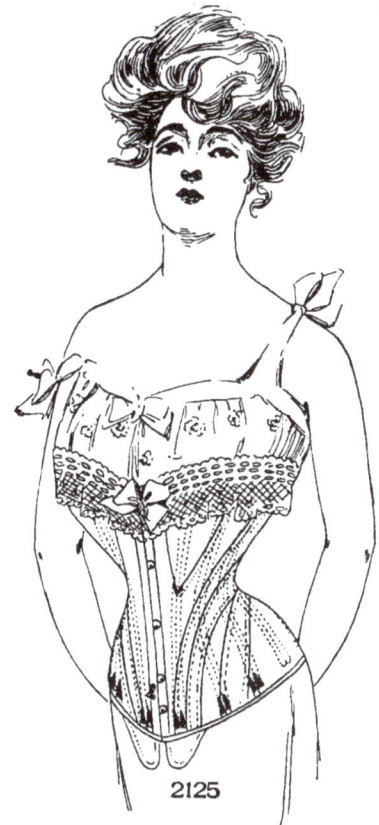

No.2125
A WHALEBONE CORSET, MADE FOR FULL FIGURES, LONG BELOW THE WAIST LINE AND MEDIUM LOW ABOVE; MADE IN WHITE AND BLACK ROMAN CLOTH. PRICE: $5.00
CHAS. A. STEVENS CATALOG 1902 (US)

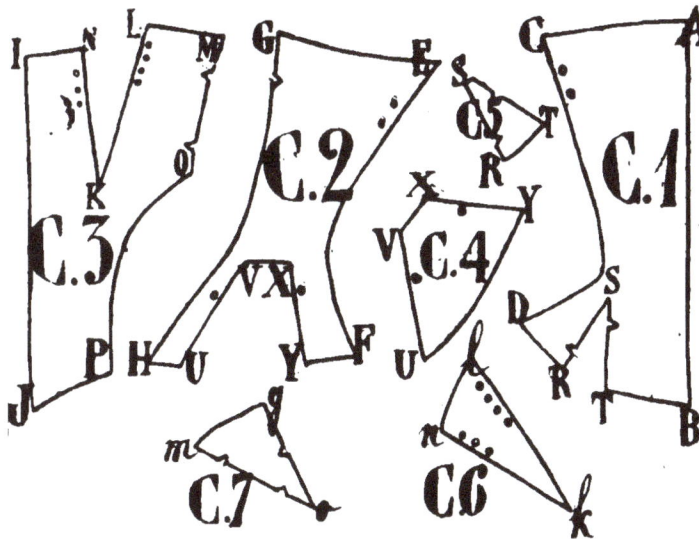

PATTERN CUTTING DIAGRAM FROM LA MODE PRATIQUE, 1899 (FRANCE)

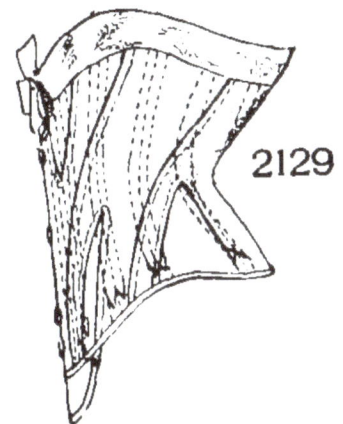

No.2129
FOR VERY FULL FIGURES, OF FINE COUTIL, IN WHITE, DRAB AND BLACK, HEAVILY FLOSSED AT BOTTOM AND BOUND TOP WITH HEAVY SATIN RIBBON; SIZES 22 TO 36. PRICE $4.00
CHAS. A. STEVENS CATALOG 1902(US)

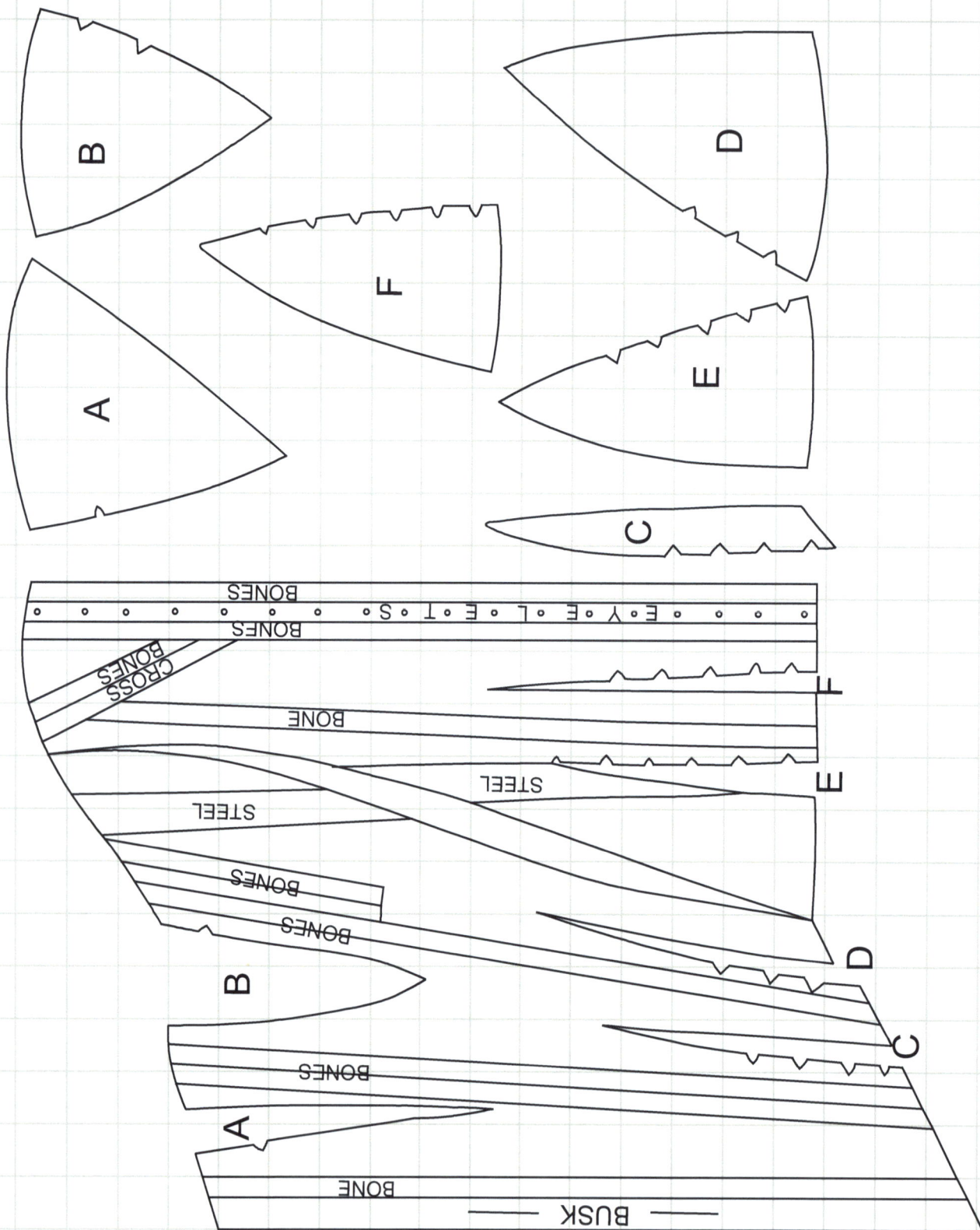

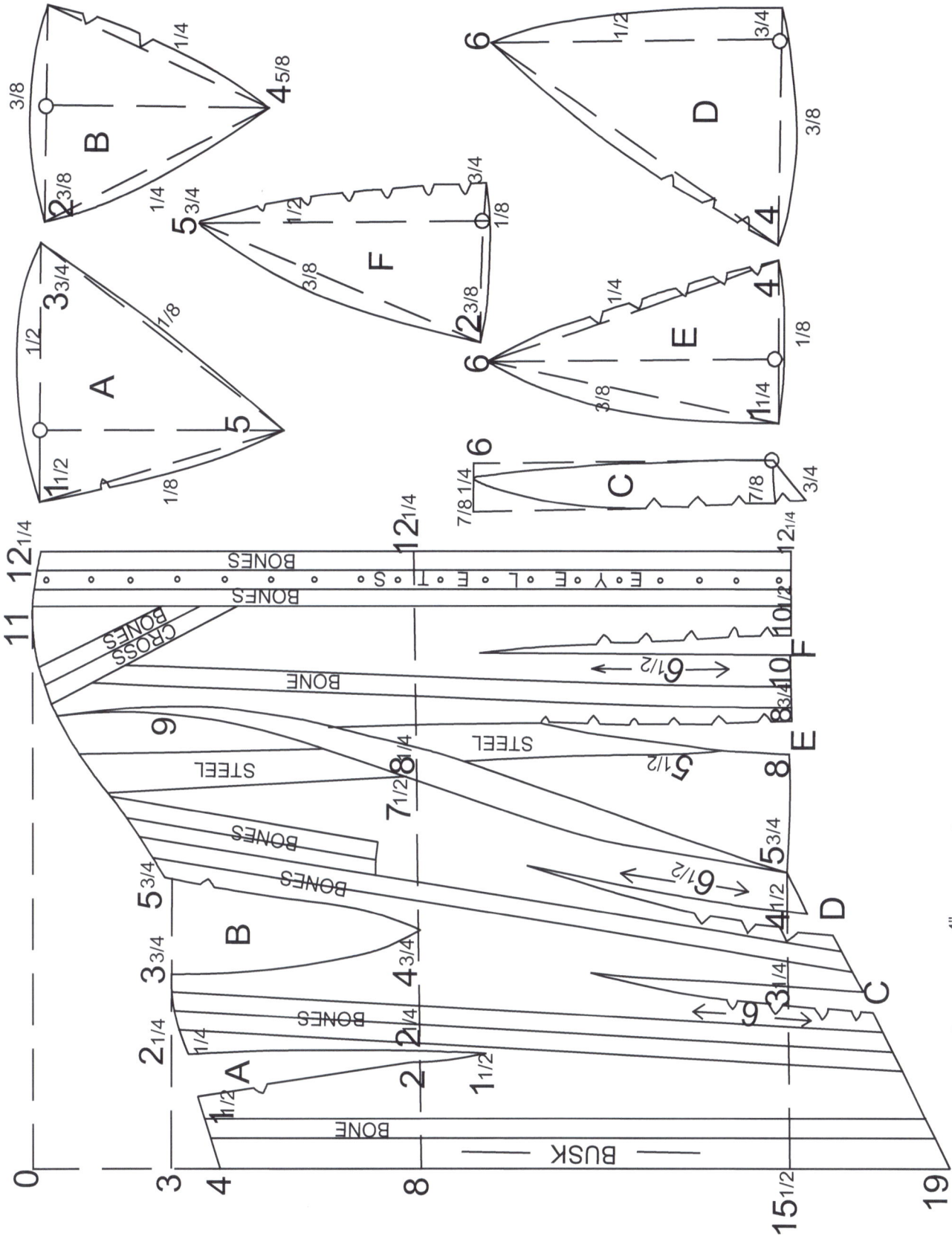

B 3/8 1/4 2 3/8 4 5/8

D 6 1/2 3/4 4 3/8

A 3 3/4 1/2 1/8 1 1/2 1/8 5

F 5 3/4 1/2 1/4 3/8 3/4 2 3/8 1/8 6

E 6 1/4 1/8 3/8 1 1/4 4

C 6 7/8 1/4 7/8 3/4

0 3 4 8 15 1/2 19

12 1/4 12 11 9 5 3/4 3 3/4 2 1/4 1 1/4 1 1/2

B **A**
BONES BONES BONE BONES STEEL BUSK

12 1/4 7 1/2 8 1/4 4 3/4 2 1/4 2 1 1/2

CROSS BONES

SOCIETY OF LADIES

12 1/4 10 1/2 10 8 3/4 10 8 5 1/2 5 3/4 4 1/2 3 1/4

F 6 1/2
E STEEL
D 6 1/2
C 6

4" 10CM

LILLIE

STRAIGHT FRONT CORSET 1902

The corset we are publishing on this page is one that is especially adapted for short stout figures, who, by its use, are very greatly improved in form.

As will be seen, the body part is cut in two pieces, there being one gusset put in over the hips, and one over the seat. The former is marked A, and the latter B.

There are two gussets inserted at the breast, C being the front one with the four notches, and D the back one with the three notches.

The making-up of this garment is on very much the same lines as we have already described. The usual busk is put down the front, bones are inserted right through the middle of the front width from the top at breast to the bottom edge. Two side steels are used. Long cross-bones are inserted over the blades to the waist at back, and two bones run from these over the seat.

Suspenders can be added either at front or hips, according to taste.

For summer wear, fine zephyrs are being used, but this being made up for stout figures the more suitable material is a strong coutil, as figures of this squatty type require more support than usual.

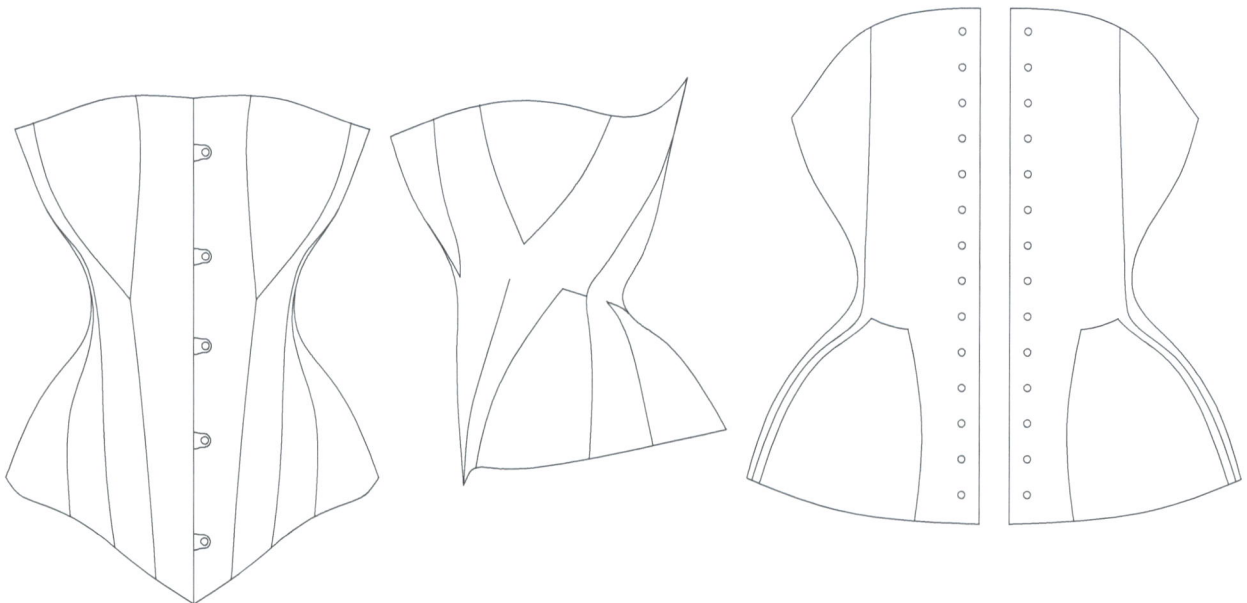

On previous pages: Lillie
Savoy Satin in English Rose, by James Hare
Lace from LaceTime on Etsy
Corset constructed by Nikki Swift, Narrowed Visions Corsets
Model, make up, hair and photography: Alivya V Free
Corset photographed by Nikki Swift

This style of corset can easily be dated to late 1901 to 1902, as the Royal Worcester Corset Co. advertised five different variations of a very similar design in their full page advertisement in the January 1902 Ladies Home Journal.

Although the pattern states that it is for the short, stout figure, examining the Royal Worcester advertisement shows how easily the design can be adapted for a wide variety of figure types, by varying the height of the corset, depth and width of the gores, and width of the sections between the gores.

While these particular catalog listings do not mention it, many corsets in this style, seen in catalogs from this year, were advertised as being bias gored. Cutting the panel and gores on the bias would allow for them to smoothly stretch over the bust and hips, resulting in a comfortable corset. The bust is low cut, allowing for support, but not compression of the bust. This loose fit of the bust was a key feature of the straight front corset:

"No bands or straps are used to constrain the figure, by which the utmost freedom and relief from pressure is sustained. With abundance of room for chest development and slight enlargement of the figure at the waist line, induced by pressure at the abdomen, which is carried unconsciously upward and downward, and by virtue of the hip spring, distributed at the sides, removing the prominence for which the straight front model is so conspicuously desired."

E. J. Weeks, President Coronet Corset Co. October 1901[33]

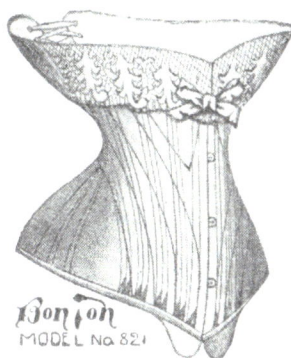

BON TON MODEL NO. 821
STRAIGHT FRONT, DESIGNED FOR SHORT STOUT FIGURES, SHORT UNDER ARM, LOW BUST AND LONG OVER HIPS AND ABDOMEN. 11-INCH FOUR-HOOK CLASP. WHITE AND DRAB IMPORTED COUTIL AND BLACK SATTEEN. SIZES 19 TO 30.

BON TON MODEL NO. 818
STRAIGHT FRONT, MEDIUM LONG UNDER ARM, LONG OVER HIP AND ABDOMEN. DESIGNED FOR TALL, FULL FIGURES. 11 1/2-INCH FIVE HOOK CLASP. COLORS, WHITE AND DRAB IMPORTED COUTIL, BLACK SATTEEN. SIZES 18 TO 30.

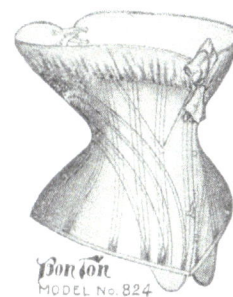

BON TON MODEL NO. 824
STRAIGHT FRONT, SHORT UNDER ARM, LOW BUST, MEDIUM LONG OVER HIPS AND ABDOMEN. DESIGNED FOR SLENDER, ALSO SMALL BUSTED, INTERMEDIATE AND HEAVY FIGURES. SIZES 18 TO 30. MADE IN WHITE, DRAB AND BLACK.
LADIES MAGAZINE, JANUARY 1902 (US)

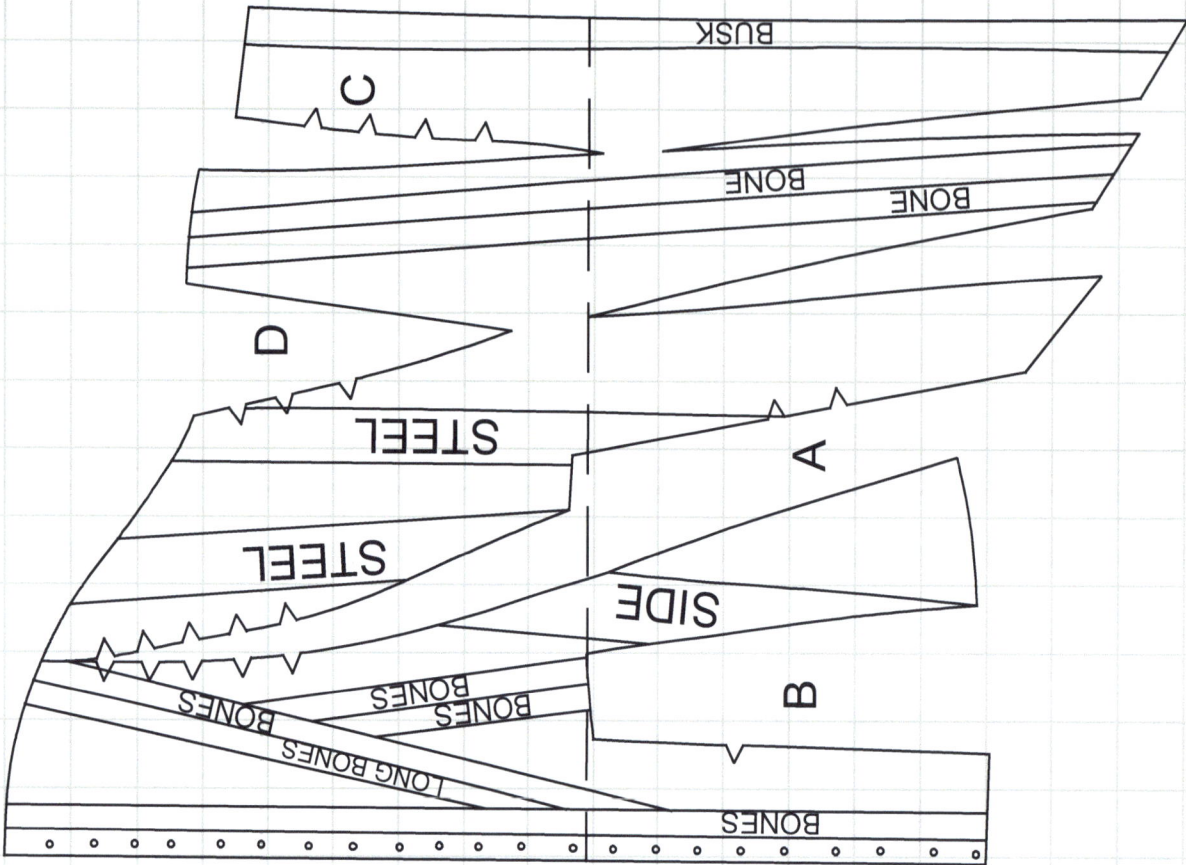

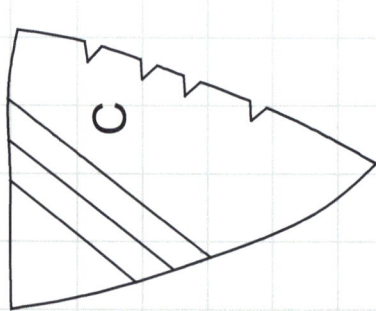

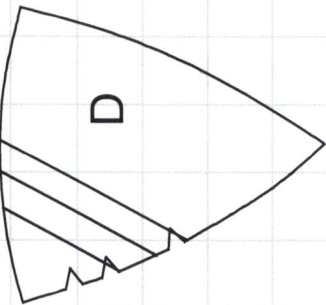

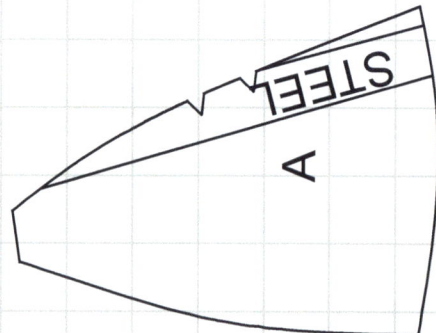

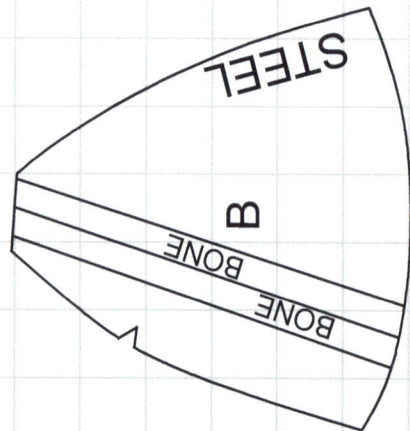

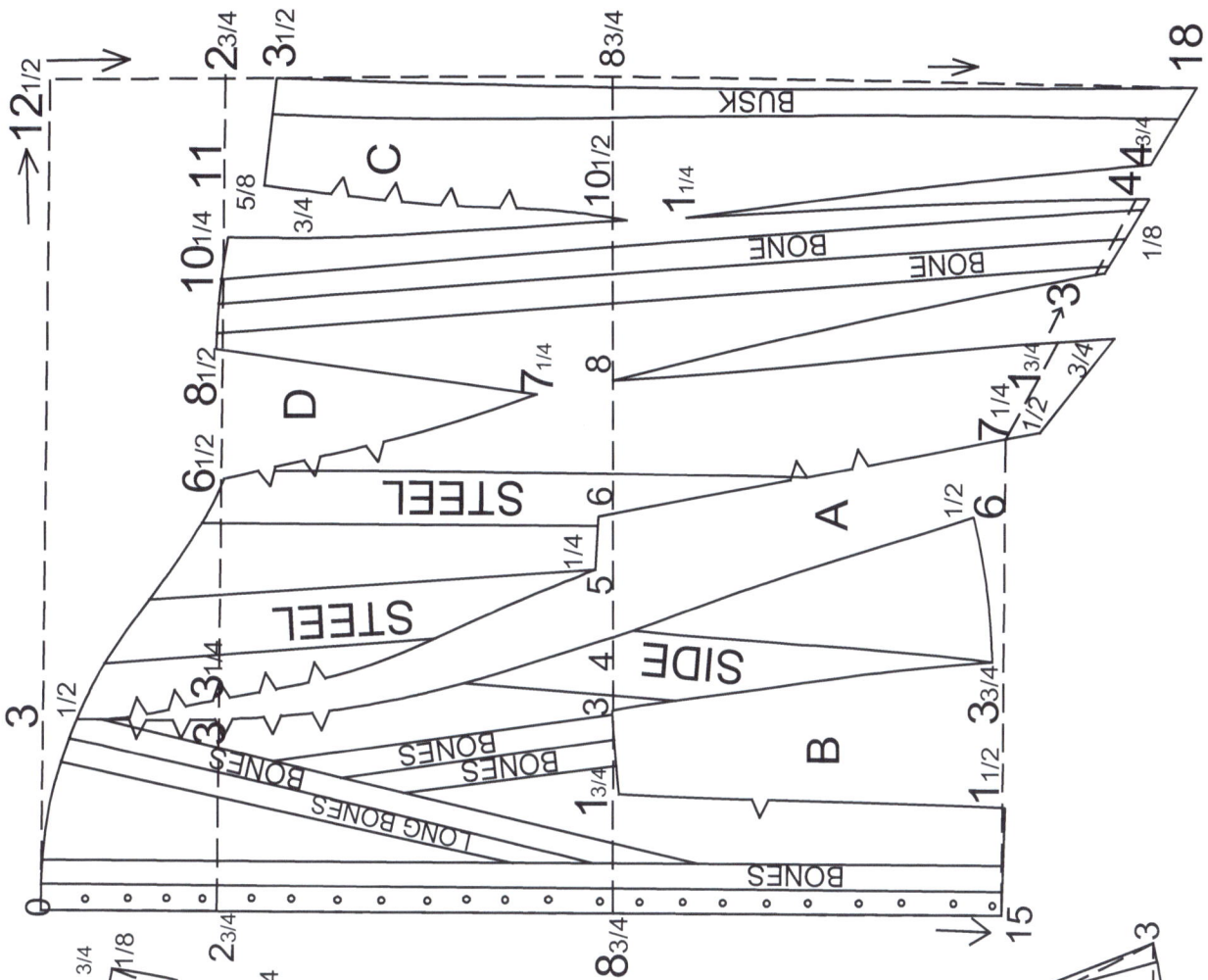

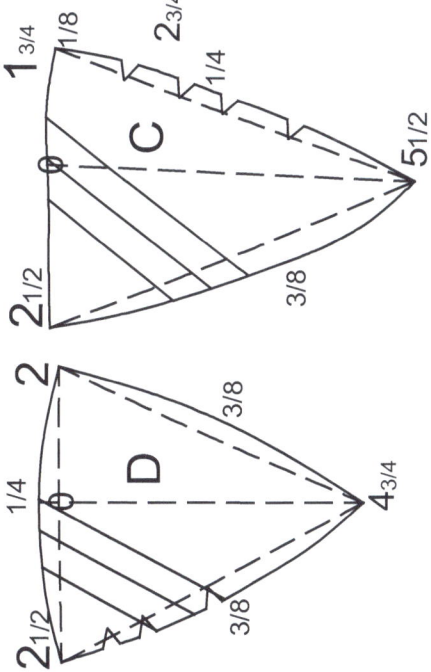

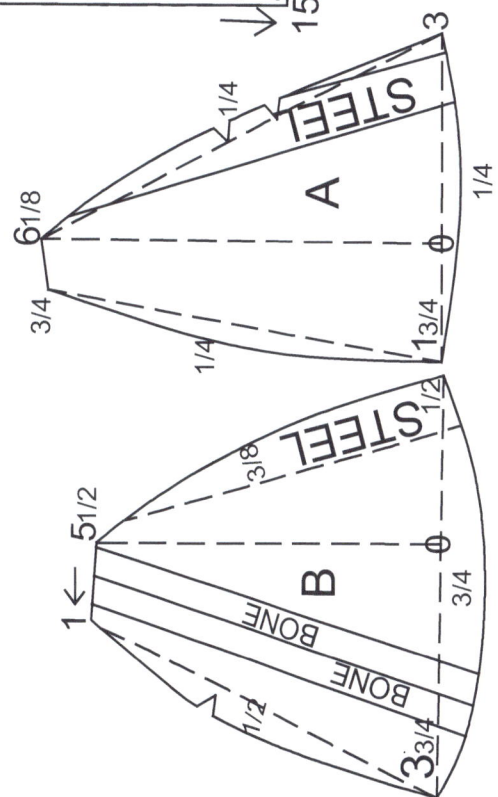

LORNA

ATHLETIC CORSET 1902

The athletic corset is an innovation which becomes an actual necessity if the fullest enjoyment is to be derived from riding, boating, cricket, golf, tennis, hockey, gymnastics, archery, cycling, dancing, motoring, racing, and many other outdoor or muscular exercises.

This corset is also highly recommended for nurses wear. For riding, boating, cycling, or any other exercise that requires a sitting posture, the corset should be cut shorter in front below the waist, and very short over the hips, as it becomes dangerous to wear it too deep below the waist for these purposes, because the busks, steels, etc., are apt to run into the wearer below the waist at the extreme edge.

This famous athletic corset is made with a piece of firm elastic webbing straight through each side, from top edge to bottom edge of corset, and is in width less at the waist than above and below; this arrangement admits of perfect freedom to the whole of the body, and will be found the most comfortable, easy, and perfect-fitting corset before the public for all outdoor exercises.

These corsets can be boned firmly, medium, half bones and drawings, or entirely boneless, excepting busks.

If the customer wishes boneless corsets, the cases which are stitched on to hold the bones, steels, etc., must be filled entirely with stitched lines from edge to edge, to fill up the tapes, 1 tick and 1/2 tick of an inch apart. Then a drawing-through needle must be procured, which is about 18 inches in length, and also a hank or two of drawing-through cotton, and with that thread the needle with a very long thread, which must be used double; draw this through each of the narrow stitched spaces; these are boneless, with the exception of busks and bones each side of eyelets.

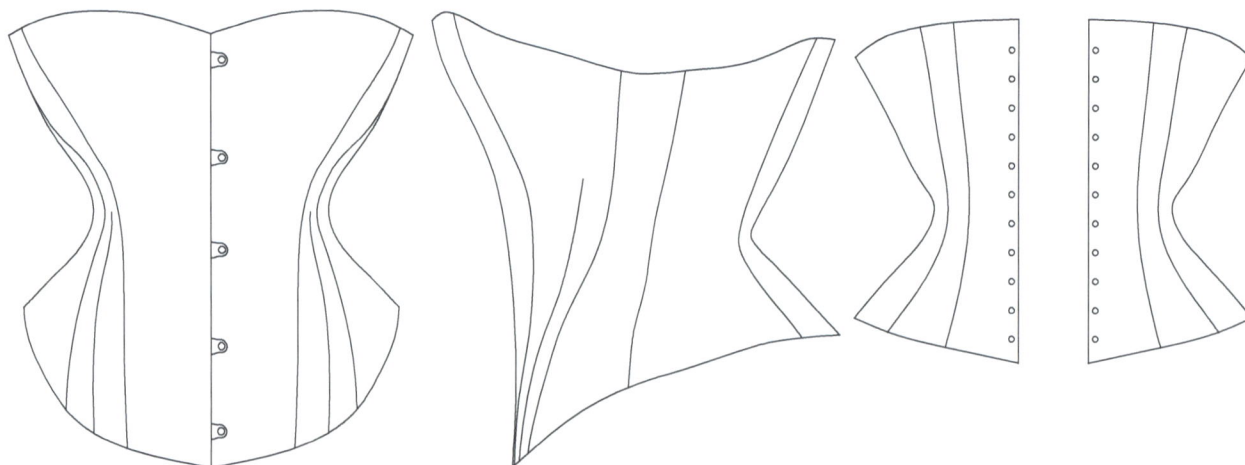

For medium firmness, stitch half of each case for a whalebone, and fill in the other half for drawing through cotton. For ordinary firm corset, bone as drafted on pattern. Elastic webbing can be had in both cotton and silk.

The well-dressed woman of the early 1900s had a large collection of corsets for many occasions, including sports. This athletic corset is noted in the description as being easy to adapt to the various needs of different sports, and is very similar in cut to an athletic corset found in Sears 1902 catalog. It is also similar to a bicycle corset, or cyclist corset, from 1895, which became fashionable when bicycling became a health craze among women in the mid-1890s.

Not all women chose to wear a special corset when they rode a bicycle, but it was certainly recommended by the fashion and sporting magazines at the time.

"Men do not dress for 'cycling as for an Easter church parade. But most women do what is just as absurd. They do not recognize any difference between trimness and tightness, between nattiness and rigidity. Not one wheelwoman in-what shall it be, wheelwomen, twenty-five or fifty – wears a bicycle corset. The ordinary corset is as uncomfortable and ungraceful on a bicycle as the corset suited to a tailored cloth dress is unsuited to a dinner-gown of tulle."[34]

W.B. Cyclist No.155 Bicycle or Riding Corset has a high hip, with elastic side sections which yield to every motion of the body, giving the wearer the most perfect ease and comfort. White, Drab, and Black. Price $1.35
Jordan Marsh Catalog, 1895
Boston (US)

No. 18T4920
Kabo Hipless Corset, medium waist, full form, made of French sateen, single strip, full boned, cut out over hip with elastic sides. Matchless for athletic purposes and comfort. No brass eyelets. Colors, white, drab or black. Sizes, 18 to 30. 95 cents
Extra sizes 31 to 36, $1.20 each
Sears 1902 catalog (US)

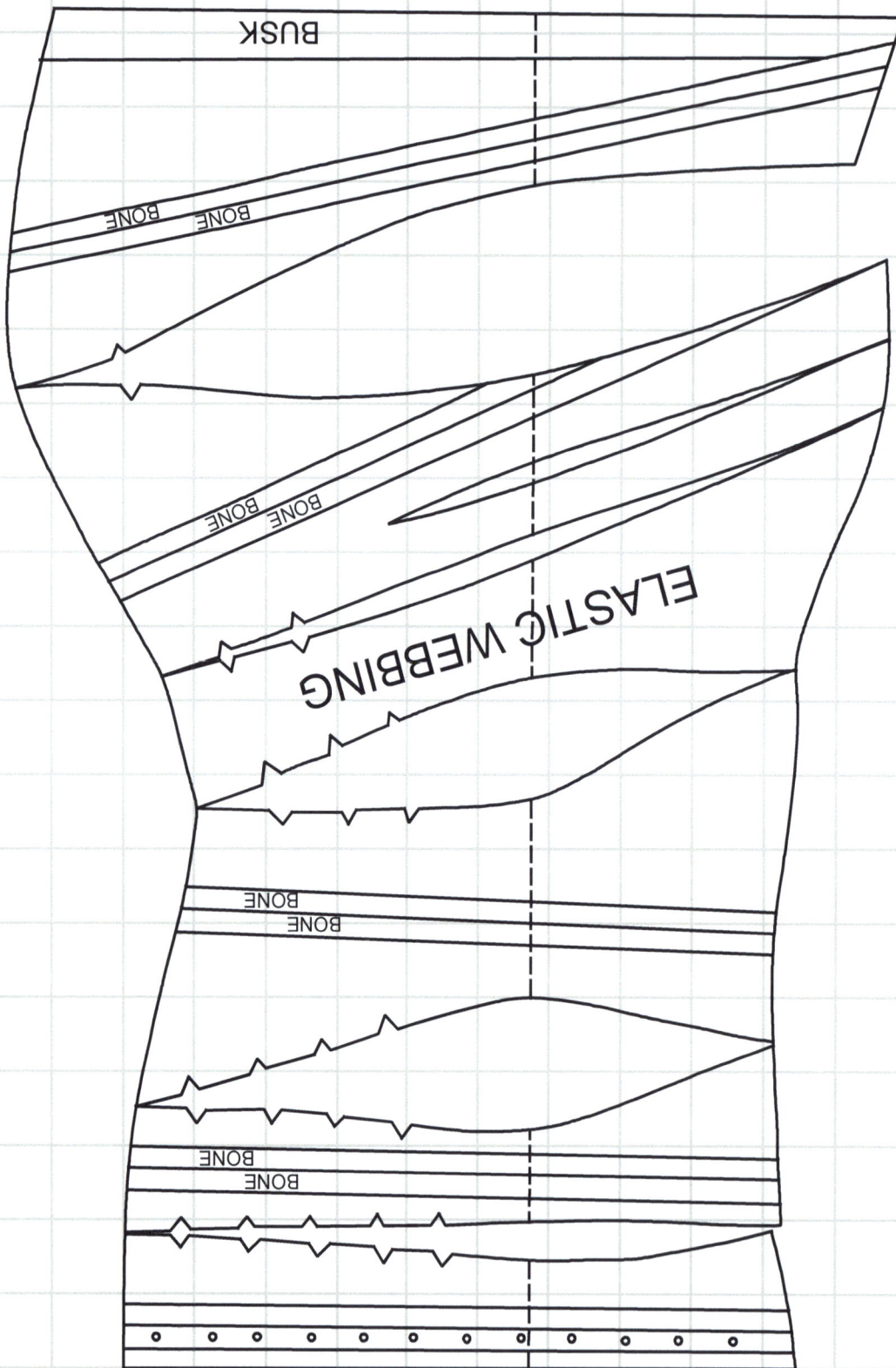

BUSK

BONE BONE

BONE BONE

ELASTIC WEBBING

BONE
BONE

BONE
BONE

4"

10CM

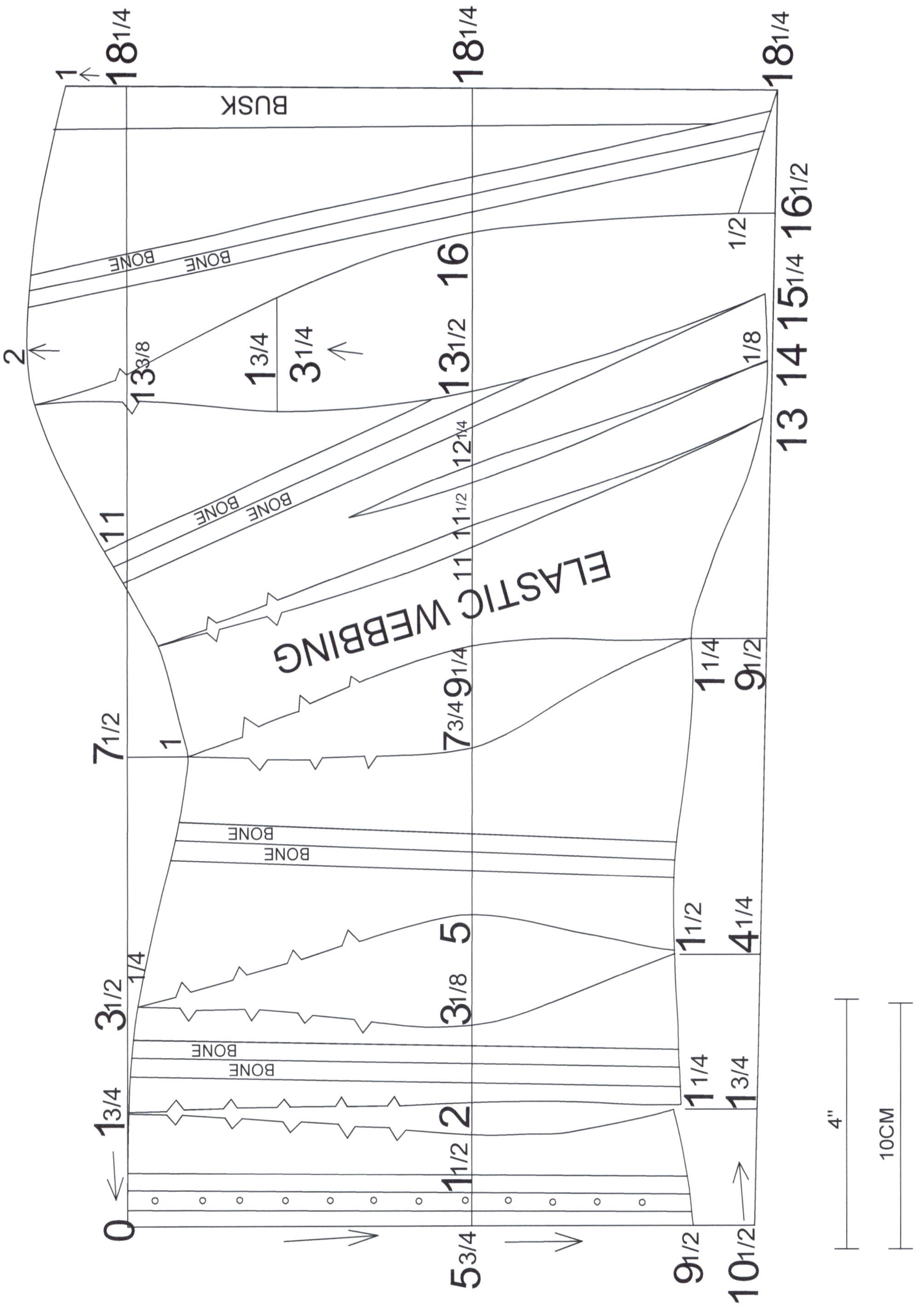

BUSK

BONE BONE

BONE BONE

ELASTIC WEBBING

BONE BONE

BONE BONE

$18^{1/4}$
$18^{1/4}$
$18^{1/4}$

$16^{1/2}$
$15^{1/4}$ $16^{1/2}$
13 14 15

1

2

$13^{3/8}$
$1^{3/4}$
$3^{1/4}$
$13^{1/2}$ 16
$12^{1/4}$
11 $11^{1/2}$
11

$1/2$

$1/8$

11

$7^{1/2}$
1
$7^{3/4}$ $9^{1/4}$

$1^{1/4}$
$9^{1/2}$

$3^{1/2}$
$1/4$

5
$3^{1/8}$

$1^{1/2}$
$4^{1/4}$

$1^{3/4}$
2

BONE
BONE

$1^{1/4}$
$1^{3/4}$

$1^{1/2}$

0

$5^{3/4}$

$9^{1/2}$
$10^{1/2}$

4"

10CM

ISOBEL

EQUESTRIENNE CORSET 1900-1904

The style of corset portrayed on the next page in diagram form is one which will appeal to those readers whose clientele includes' ladies who desire to ride occasionally. It is adapted to both promenade or equestrienne purposes, being fitted with an elastic webbing sidegore, which provides for the forward bending attitude adopted by a majority of riders.

The material mostly favoured is coutil, although almost any material could be adopted.

The notches show how the pattern goes together, and in all there are 12 parts, including two elastic gores and three wedge portions, which latter are inserted as indicated by letters A on back B and C at breast.

There are not a great many bones used, owing to the fact that extra pliability is produced by the elastic sides; but should more be required they may be inserted in centre of back gore, over wedge-piece, and between the front set of bones. The various parts must be cut from the straight of the material, so as to avoid stretching, and the elastic must be of good thickness, and well woven and covered, as the best quality is almost unaffected by the heat of the body.

It will be noticed that steels are conspicuous by their absence, owing to their unsuitability to such shapes where extra expansion and pliability are absolutely necessary.

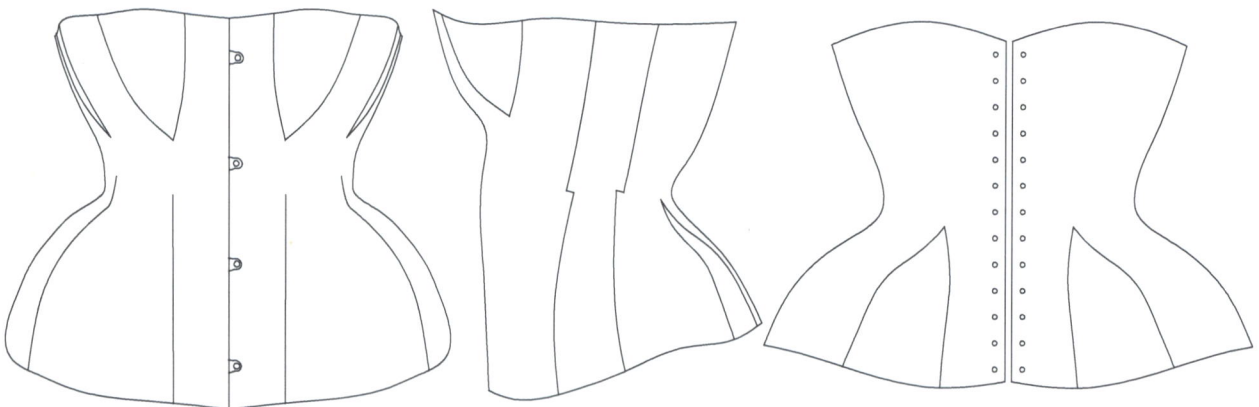

This equestrian, or riding, corset, dates to 1900-1904, based on the cut and use of gores to achieve the fashionable shape. Riding corsets were a niche market, and were not available in standard middle-class mail order catalogs.

Elizabeth Karr in her 1890 book "The American Horsewoman", gave this advice about the appropriate shape for a riding corset, and suggested a ready made corset which was easily available.

"The corset is indispensable to the elegant fit required in a riding habit, but should never be tight. It should be short on the sides and in the front and back. [...] The C.P. la Sirene [made in Paris] is undoubtedly the best corset for riding purposes for it is short, light and flexible, and not prejudicial to the ease and elegance of good riding, as is the case with the stiff, long-bodied corset."[35]

Riding corsets, and the habits worn over them, followed the shape of fashionable women's suits. Alice Hays in 1903 offered this advice, which applies to this style of equestrian corset:

"Before trying [a riding coat] on, its wearer should procure a good pair of riding corsets, which must allow for free play to the movements of her hips and above all she must not lace tightly. Wasp waists have luckily gone out, never, I hope, to return. The size of a woman's waist, if she is not deformed, is in proportion to that of the rest of her body. Therefore a pinched waist, besides rendering the tightly girthed-up lady uncomfortable, to say nothing of its probable effect on the tint of her nose, deceives no one. It is impossible to ride with ease and grace in tight stays ..."[36]

C.P. LA SIRENE CORSET, 1885-1890 MET MUSEUM, ACC. NO. 2003.133A

MISS BURNABY ON BUTTERFLY, WEARING A FASHIONABLE RIDING HABIT 1901-03 FROM "THE HORSEWOMAN" P.9

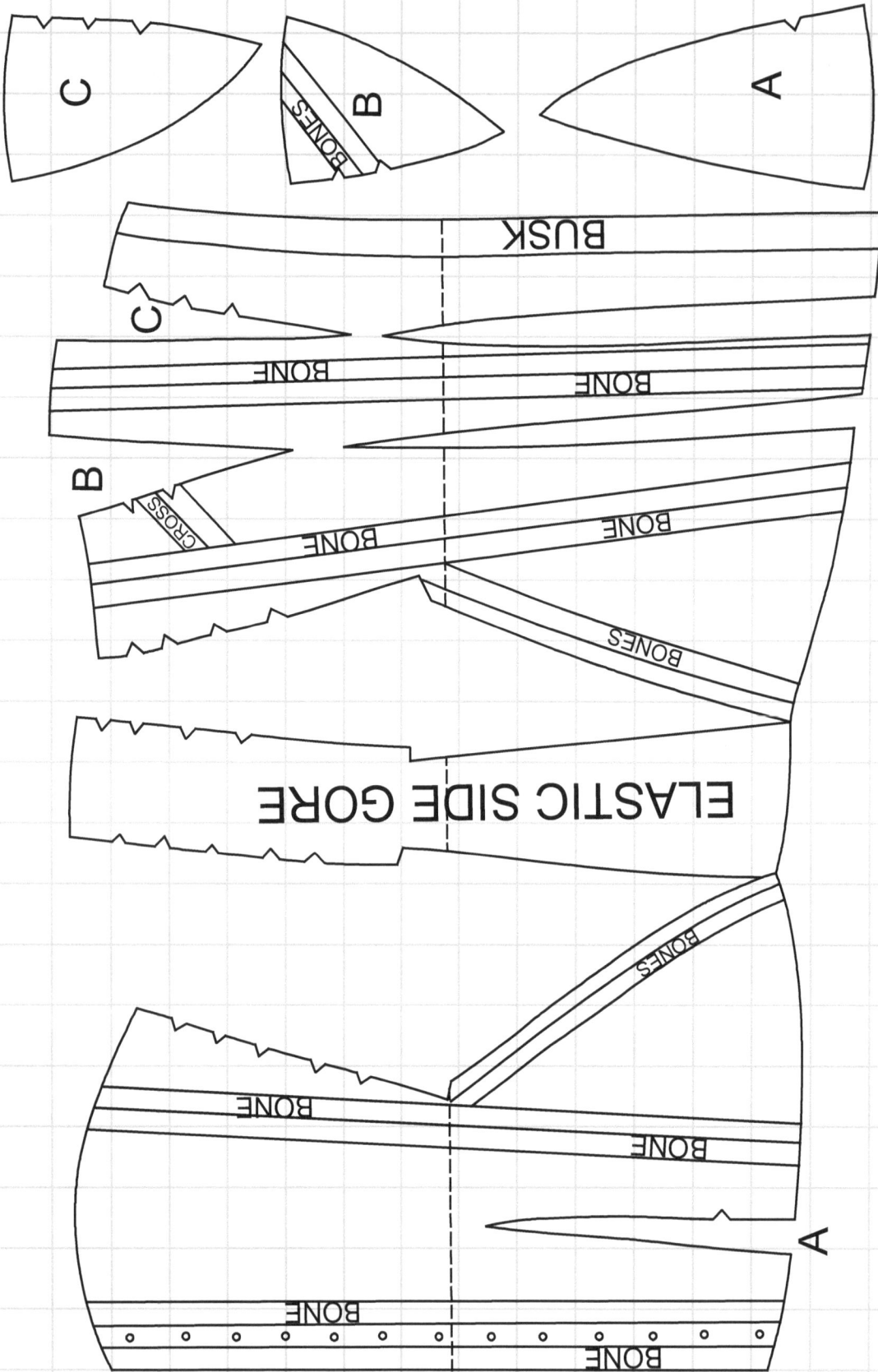

C

B

BONES

A

BUSK

C

BONE

BONE

B

CROSS

BONE

BONE

BONES

ELASTIC SIDE GORE

BONES

BONE

BONE

A

BONE

BONE

4"

10CM

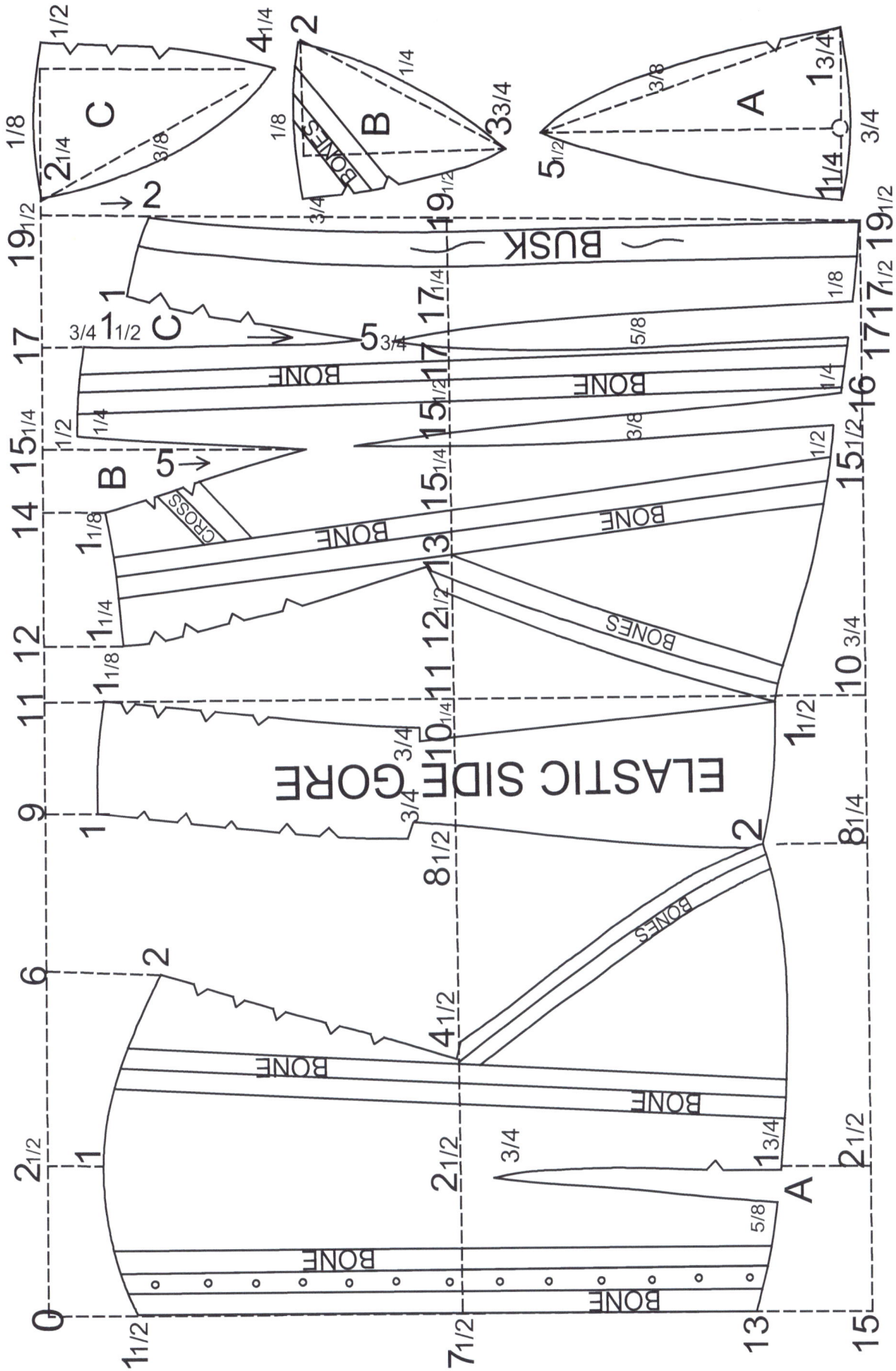

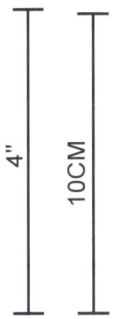

HELENE

PARISIAN ONE PIECE CORSET 1905-1906

The diagram on the following page gives a reduced model of a corset cut from one piece, and illustrates where the bones may be placed to obtain the best results.

The suppressions between the various parts must be adapted to the requirements of the figure, and the height above the waist as well as the length below it must be regulated in harmony with the customer's tastes.

The amount taken out between 3 1/2 and 6 1/4 is governed by the prominence of the seat, the quantities suppressed at 7 1/2 and 8 3/4 ; 10 1/4 and 11 1/2 is regulated by the size of the hips, and the ,quantity taken out at 14 and 15 3/4 by the prominence of the bust. This draft is suitable for a 36 breast, 22 waist, and 38 seat, and other sizes may be drafted by using a graduated tape agreeing with the half chest measure.

On previous pages: Helene
Savoy Satin in Celestial Blue, by James Hare
Lace from LaceTime on Etsy
Corset constructed by Nikki Swift, Narrowed Visions Corsets
Model, make up, hair and photography: Alivya V Free

This corset is highly unusual as it is cut from a single piece, with the shaping provided only by vertical darts, leaving the top and bottom edge of the fabric unbroken. A corset with a similar cut, but made from specially woven elastic was patented in France in December of 1905, and published in Les Dessous Elegants in July 1906. [37]

No. 357,545 Corset élastique en une seul piece. M. Emile Morin résident in France. Publié le 30 decembre 1905.

La présente invention est relativé à un corset élastique caractérisé par des parties constitutives spéciales formées de bandes de tricot dimunuées au métier et permettant d'obtenir ce corset d'une seule piéce. Cette invention va êtra décrite ci-aprés en référence au dessin annexé, dans lequel.

No. 357,545 Elastic corset in one piece. Mr. Emile Morin resident of France. Published on December 30, 1905.

The present invention is relative to an elastic corset characterized by special constituent parts formed of knitted strips separated on the loom and making it possible to obtain this corset of a single piece. This invention is described below in the accompanying figures.

In the original pattern, no particular fabric or material is mentioned, so this corset could have been intended to be cut from elastic, or any other fabric. A firmly woven cotton/silk blend satin has been chosen for the reproduction corset seen on the previous pages.

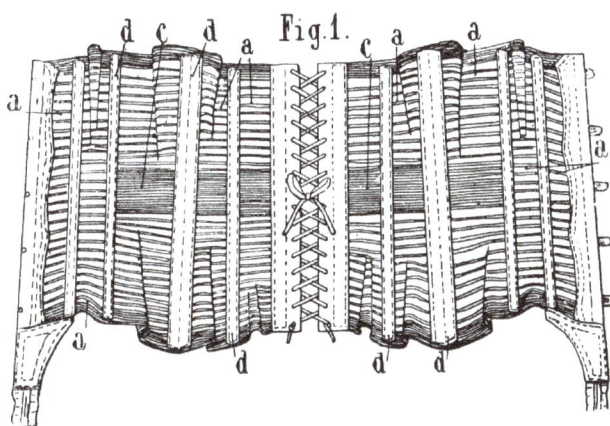

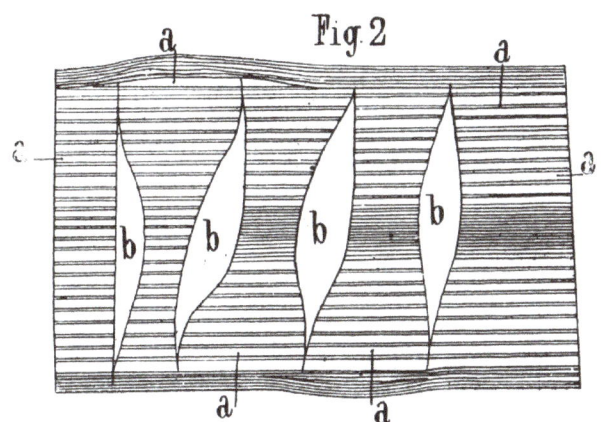

DIAGRAMS FROM FRENCH PATENT NO. 357,545 ELASTIC CORSET IN ONE PIECE

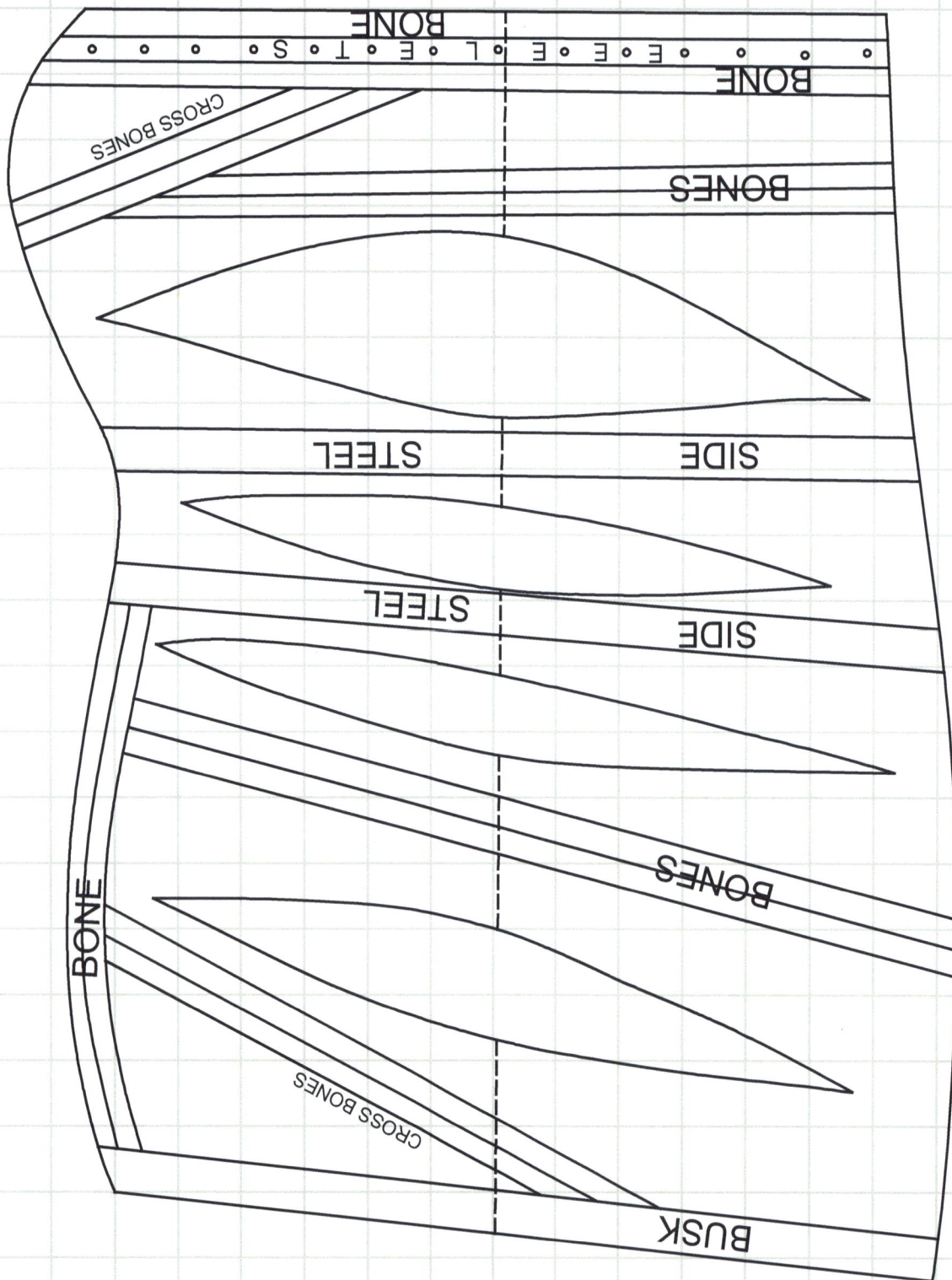

BONE

BONE

EYELETS

CROSS BONES

BONES

STEEL

SIDE

STEEL

SIDE

BONE

BONES

CROSS BONES

BUSK

4"

10CM

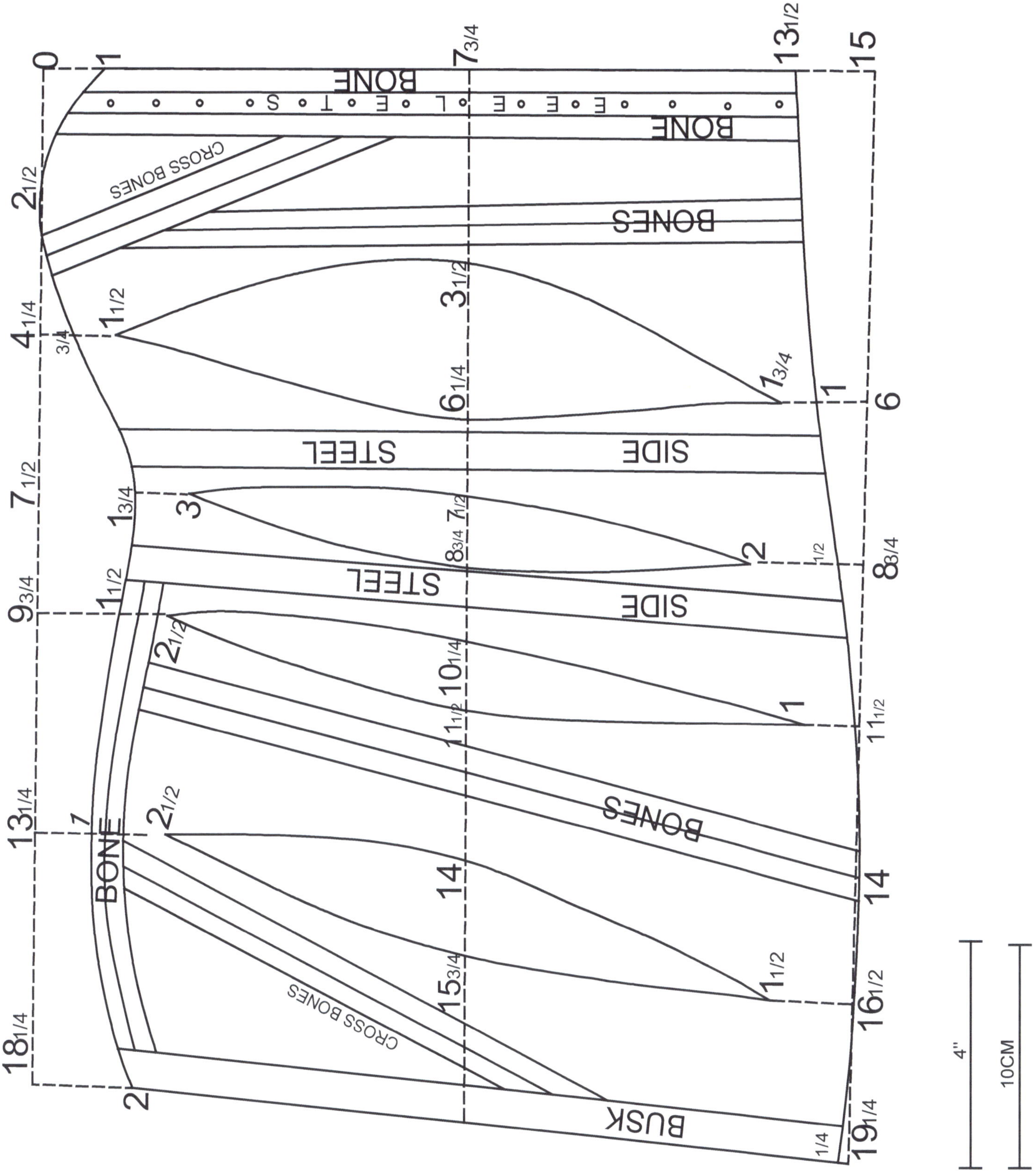
BONE
S E T T E E L S
BONE
CROSS BONES
BONES
STEEL
SIDE
STEEL
SIDE
BONES
BONE
CROSS BONES
BUSK
4"
10CM

OLIVE

MATERNITY CORSET 1904-1908

We next deal with a few of the special styles of corsets required for different purposes. The most important of these is what is generally known as the maternity corset, which requires several special features embodied in them.

They have to be capable of considerable adaptation, as, owing to the constantly changing form of the wearer they must be altered accordingly.

In the first stages of maternity the corset must be made to meet up the back to within half-an-inch.

They must be open through each side, and, consequently, boned and eyeletted at each edge to admit of the necessary letting-out or taking in at the different parts from time to time, and a 4-inch tab of facing of material placed right through under the side facings.

The fronts should be cut as straight as possible, for the simple reason that the less curve there is imparted to them the less the condition of the wearer is apparent.

The fronts should not be too deep, because, as the size increases, there is a tendency for the bottom of the fronts to stick away from the figure, and so produce a very objectionable appearance.

Special attention must also be given to avoid all undue pressure under the bosom; indeed sufficient provision should be made for the breasts to drop well into the corsets.

The reduced model given on the following page is a splendid example of the maternity corset, for they are as adaptable to the last stages as the first, keeping the figure as trim and neat as could be desired, either for the outer world or the friends at home.

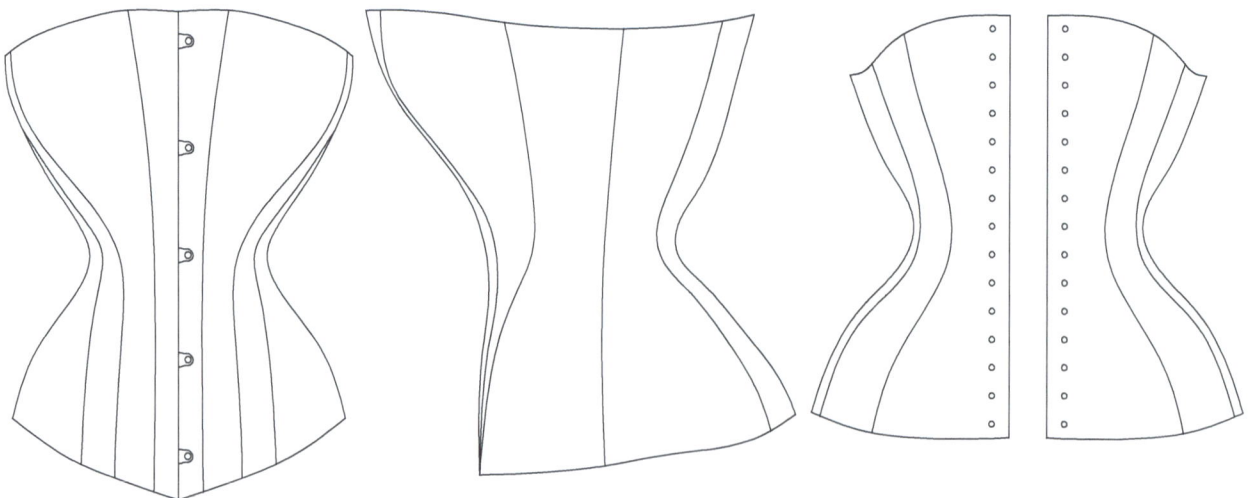

To cut, place the straightest edge of each piece to straight of material on the double; the straight edge of each piece is the most pointed edge at the bottom.
Instructions for tapes and bones have already been given, as well as finishing, etc.

Maternity corsets were not, as a rule, used to reduce the appearance of pregnancy, but to support the bust, and to help support the stomach muscles which would have been under-developed due to the wearing of a corset from an early age. Even in the current era, where stomach muscles are usually well developed in women, doctors sometimes prescribe the wearing of a pregnancy support belt to help relieve the strain on the stomach muscles. While nursing corsets are easy to find in early catalogs, illustrations of maternity corsets can be hard to find prior to 1907, except for the rare advertisement in ladies magazines. Thankfully, maternity corsets followed the general shape of the fashion corsets, which helps to date this corset to 1904-1908. The high bust would have supported the increased size of the breasts due to pregnancy, and the side-lacings would have adjusted over the course of the pregnancy to support the increased weight of the baby. Hose supporters may have been sewn on afterwards to hold up the stockings, as stocking garters worn at the top of the calf were not recommended by doctors, as it would impact the blood flow to the lower legs and lead to swelling.

While the pattern indicates the use of a busk, many of the advertisements for maternity corsets show a soft button front. The H&W maternity waist shown below, has a soft button front, shoulder straps, removable steels and buttons at the side to attach garters, which would support the stockings. A maternity corset, dated 1909, uses a busk for closure, but appears to have an elastic section at the front.

Grand Prize St. Louis 1904

H&W MATERNITY WAIST SOFT AND PLIABLE, WITH LACINGS ON EACH SIDE WHICH CAN BE ADJUSTED TO THE COMFORT OF THE WEARER, ALL STEELS REMOVABLE. THIS WAIST HOLDS THE FIGURE AT ALL TIMES IN THE PROPER POSTION, BRINING PHYSICAL AND MENTAL COMFORT. IT IS A BOON TO THE EXPECTANT MOTHER. PRICE $1.50
THE LADIES HOME JOURNAL, MARCH 1908 (US)

MATERNITY CORSET DESIGNED TO GIVE HEALLHFUL SUPPORT AND PRESENTABLENESS.
PRICES, $4.00, 6.00, 10.00 AND 15.00
WOOLNOUGH-CORSETIERS
1909-1910 (US)

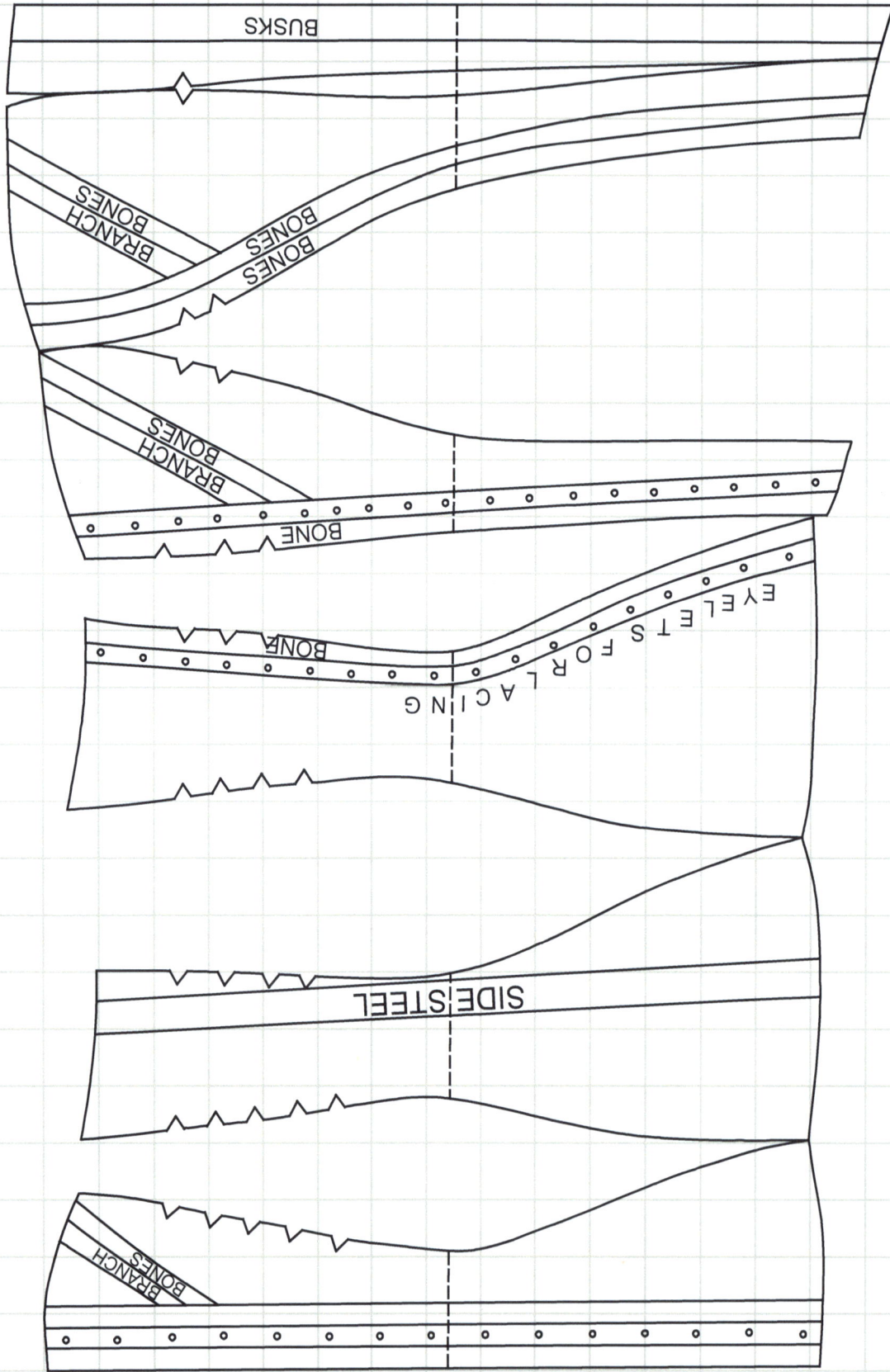

BUSKS

BRANCH BONES

BONES

BONES

BRANCH BONES

BONE

BONE

EYELETS FOR LACING

SIDE STEEL

BRANCH BONES

4"

10CM

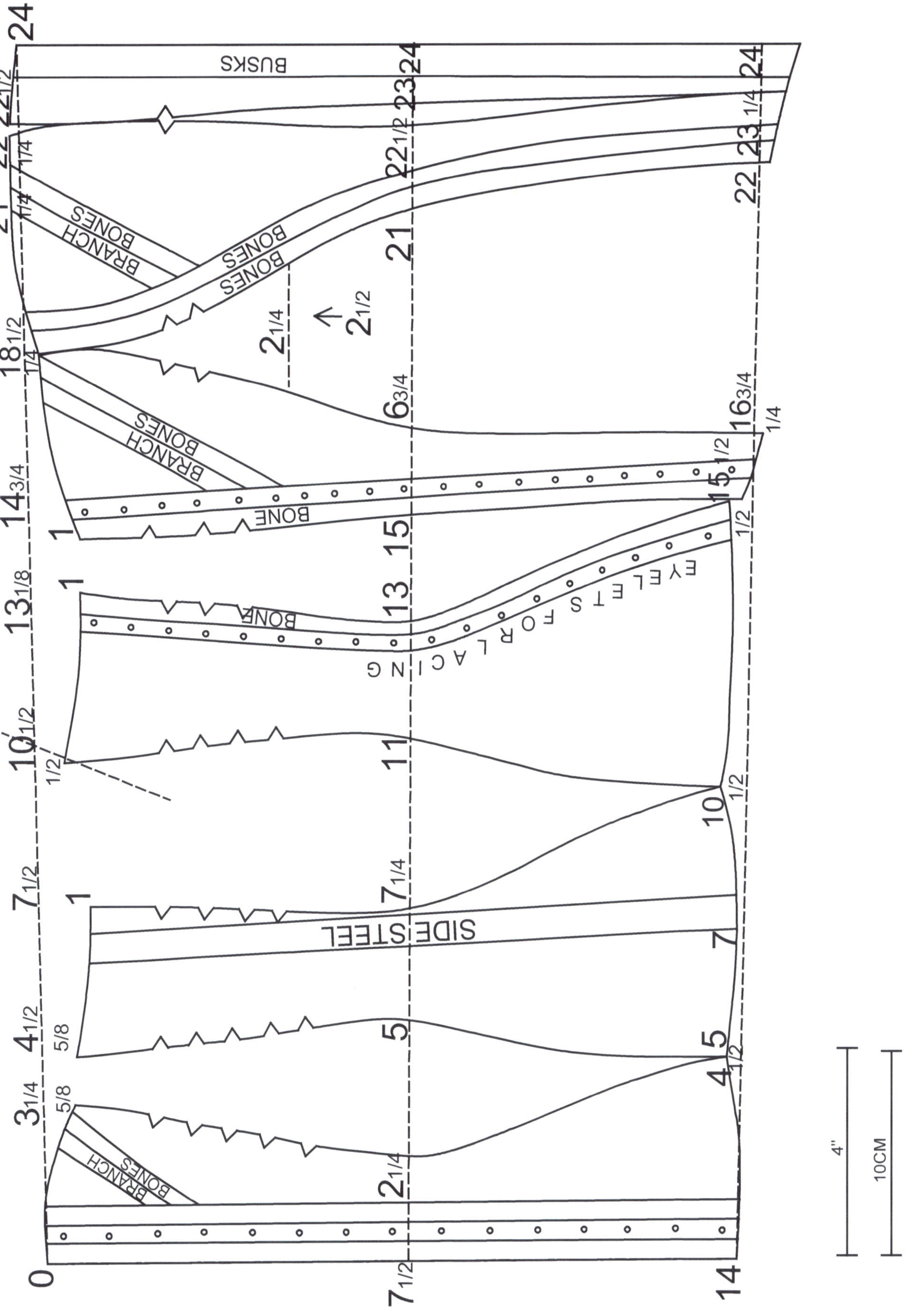

24

24

BUSKS

22 1/2

22 22 1/2

22 1/4

23 24

21

1/4

BRANCH BONES

BONES

BONES

22 1/2

21

23 1/4

23

18 1/2

1/4

2 1/4

2 1/2

22

BRANCH BONES

6 3/4

14 3/4

1

BONE

15

16 3/4

15 1/2

1/4

13 1/8

1

BONE

13

E Y E L E T S   F O R   L A C I N G

15 1/2

10

1/2

10 1/2

1/2

11

10

1/2

7 1/2

1

SIDE STEEL

7 1/4

7

4 1/2

5/8

5

4 5

1/2

3 1/4

5/8

BRANCH BONES

2 1/4

0

7 1/2

14

4"

10CM

MADELINE

NURSING CORSET 1902-1908

One of the first things a lady has to study upon getting up and about again after accouchement, is the corset which is to be worn during the time of nursing, to admit of giving convenience for suckling, and to assist in bringing back the figure to its natural symmetry and proportions. To do this, the corset must be nice and straight in front, so as to prevent the stomach from rising and becoming high, which is very distressing and objectionable to women who study their figure, appearance, carriage, and comfort, and do not care to look unsightly before their friends in the outer world. Nursing corsets should be cut and made with the bosom part to lace through or button, which ever is preferred.

The bosoms should in no way be tightened, as that is, in all cases, apt to flatten the natural figure, and render a flat-looking, disproportionate and ugly appearance after the time of suckling is over.

Nursing corsets, when new, should not meet through (down) the back, at any rate when first beginning to wear, and should be comfortably laced to within 2 1/2 to 3 inches. It is essential that they be allowed very well open, so has to allow the wearer to gradually increase the tightness, to get the figure back again to its usual proportions of size, ease, and symmetry of form.

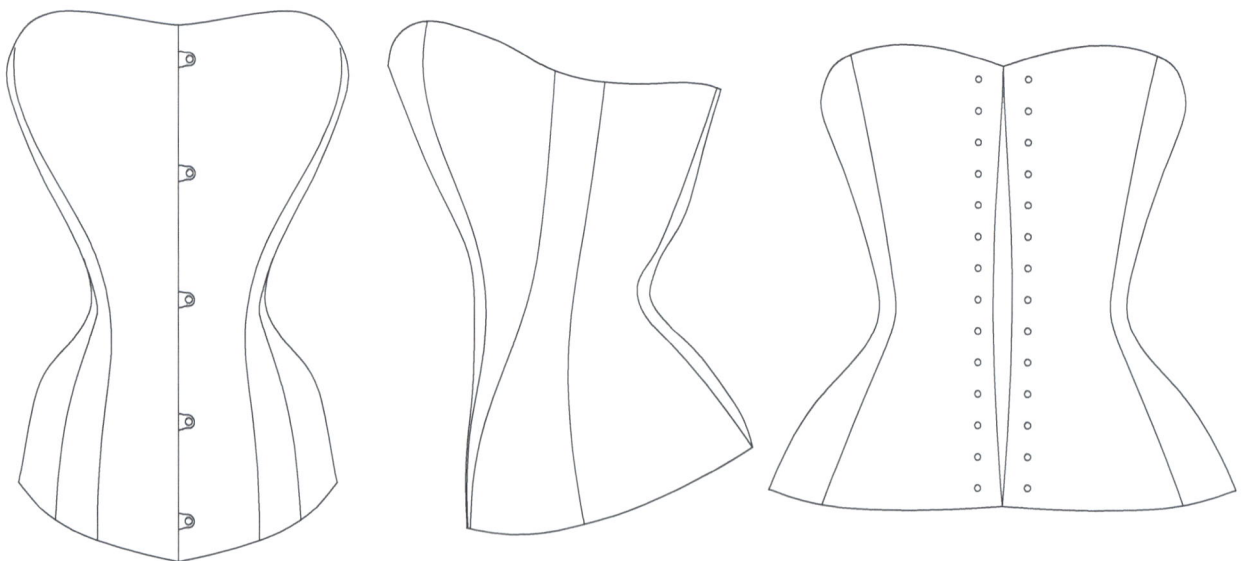

Nursing corsets, like maternity corsets, in general followed the style lines of fashionable corsets. However they were adapted for easy access to the breasts for nursing and had better bust support than most fashionable corsets. Some also had side lacing to help the new mother as she regained her figure.

While this corset pattern calls for a laced or buttoned seam, the most common solution for breast access seen in US and Canadian catalogs is to have an open cutout covered by a buttoned or snapped flap, as seen in the examples here.

Even at the height of the straight front, bias gore style (1901-1908), the styling of nursing corsets remained quite old-fashioned, and favored the older, striped style, with external boning channels and straight seams. Common fabrics were jean or coutil, in drab or white.

Similar corsets were sold from 1902-1909 with small variations in the shaping of the bottom edge and the height of the bust.

S.R. & CO'S NURSING CORSET, FIVE HOOK REINFORCED CLASP. MADE OF GOOD CORSET JEANS, BONED BUST, STRONG JEANS GIRDLE, TWO SIDE STEELS. COLOR DRAB ONLY. SIZES 18-30, 75¢
SEARS CATALOG, 1902 (US)

R2-53. NURSING, MEDIUM WAIST, SINGLE STRIP OF SATEEN, WHITE AND DRAB, 18-30. 1.25
EATON'S CATALOG, 1904
(CANADA)

COMFORTABLE NURSING CORSET, NO.18K230
"MOTHERS' FRIEND" NURSING CORSET, FOUR-HOOK, REINFORCED CLASP. MADE OF GOOD QUALITY COUTIL. BONED BUST, STRONG JEAN GIRDLE, TWO SIDE STEELS. COLORS, DRAB OR WHITE. SIZES 18 TO 30 INCHES. PRICE 77¢
SEARS CATALOG #117, 1908 (US)

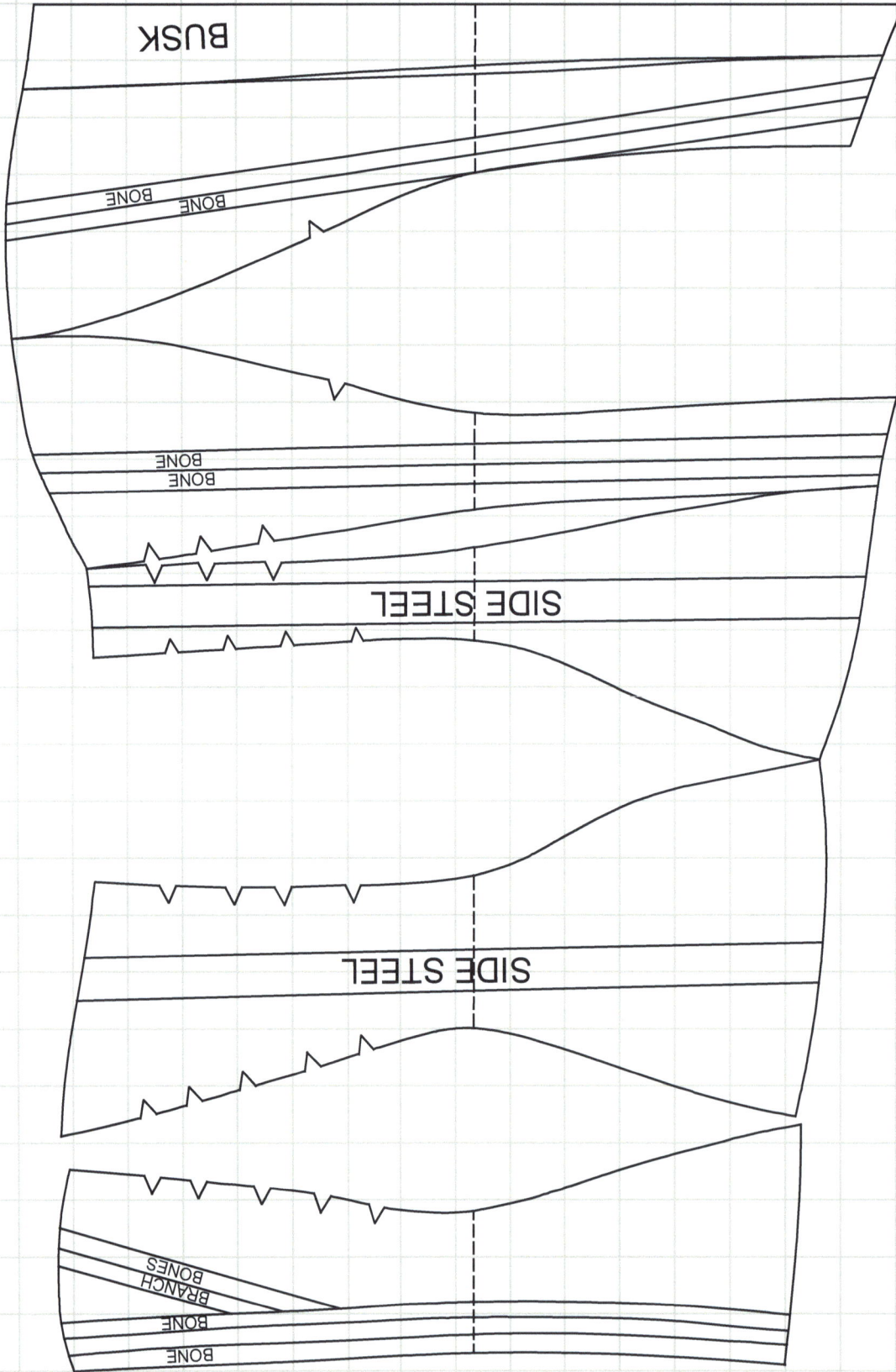

BUSK

BONE
BONE
BONE

BONE
BONE

SIDE STEEL

SIDE STEEL

BRANCH
BONES
BONE
BONE

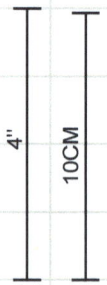

4"

10CM

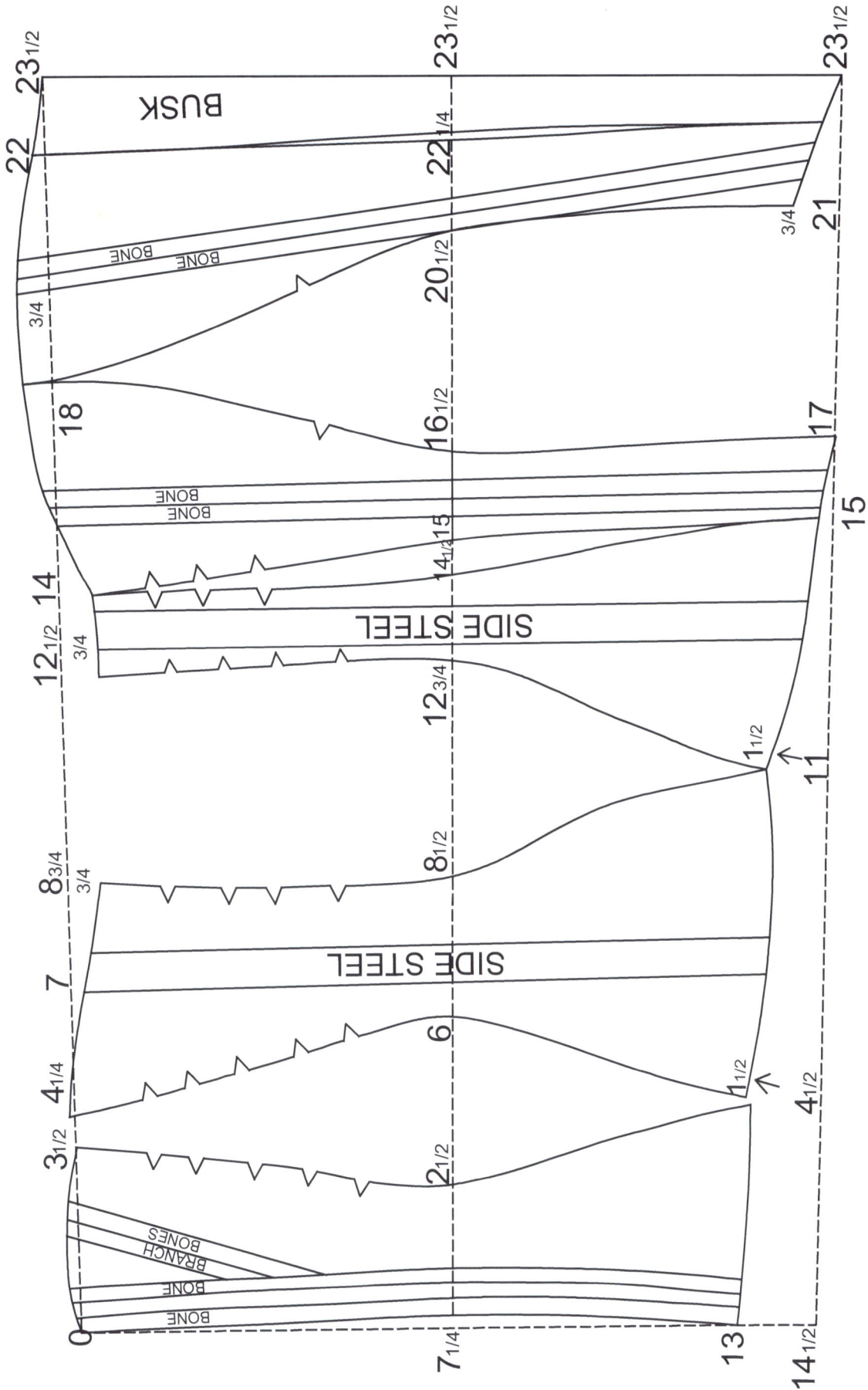

BUSK

BONE
BONE
3/4

BONE
BONE

SIDE STEEL

SIDE STEEL

BONE
BRANCH
BONES
BONE

23½   23½   23½
22   22¼
3/4   21
3/4
20½
18   16½   17
14½15   15
14   12¾
12½   3/4
1½   11
8¾   8½
3/4
7
6   1½   4½
4¼
3½   2½   4½
0
7¼
13
14½

4"

10CM

MILLIE

BELTED CORSET 1907

A very practical type of corset for corpulent figures is the one shown on this page. The lower parts of the side gores are all cut in the form of a straight band, and this may be either of the same material as the rest of the corset or it may be of elastic. The notches clearly show how the parts go together, as well as illustrating that the steels and bones are continued through to the bottom. In all other respects the diagram is self-explanatory, and it will be a very simple matter to vary the height above the waist in harmony with the customer's wishes.

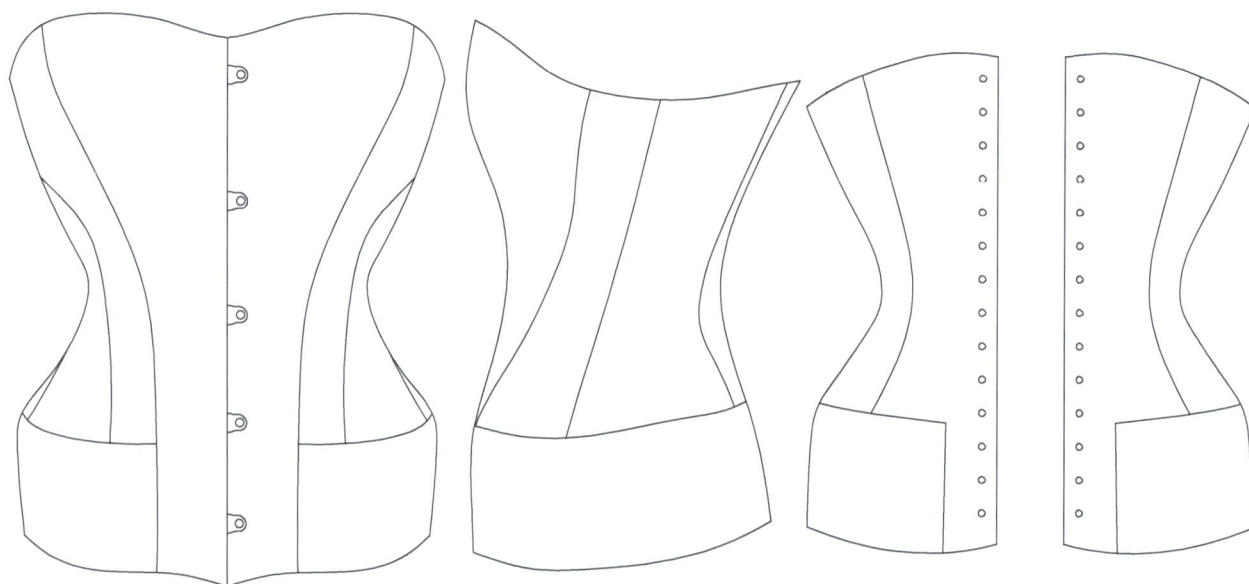

The very straight lower edge of this corset pattern firmly dates it to post 1905, when the bias cut French style with shaping gores began to be replaced by the older strip panel style cut, which was popular pre-1900.

Corsets with a straight grain piece at the hip, commonly referred to as a belt, were designed to help control and reduce a larger lower abdomen and prevent the lower edge of the corset from being stretched out during wear.

Earlier examples with this feature, such as the mid-1880s Pretty Housemaid corset[38], had a stiffened, corded section for the belt, such as the 1907 Vendome Belted Corset appears to have. A spoon busk, which is a much stiffer busk than a standard straight busk, is seen in both of the advertisements below, and adds to the ability of the corset to flatten the lower abdomen.

S&S VENDOME BELTED CORSET
SPOON BUSK 13" VENDOME, BELTED FOR STOUT
FIGURES, REAL WHALEBONE (SEE ILLUSTRATION) WHITE:
10/9 BLACK 12/6 IN WHITE AND BLACK
1907 ARMY NAVY STORES CATALOGUE (UK)

BELTED CORSET, DESIGNED TO AVOID COMPRESSION ON
THE UPPER AND LOWER ABDOMEN, AND IN CASE OF A
MOBILE KIDNEY, CAN BE FITTED WITH PADS TO SUPPORT
THE KIDNEY.
1907 CATALOGUE DE CORSETS DE RAINAL FRÈRES
(FRANCE)

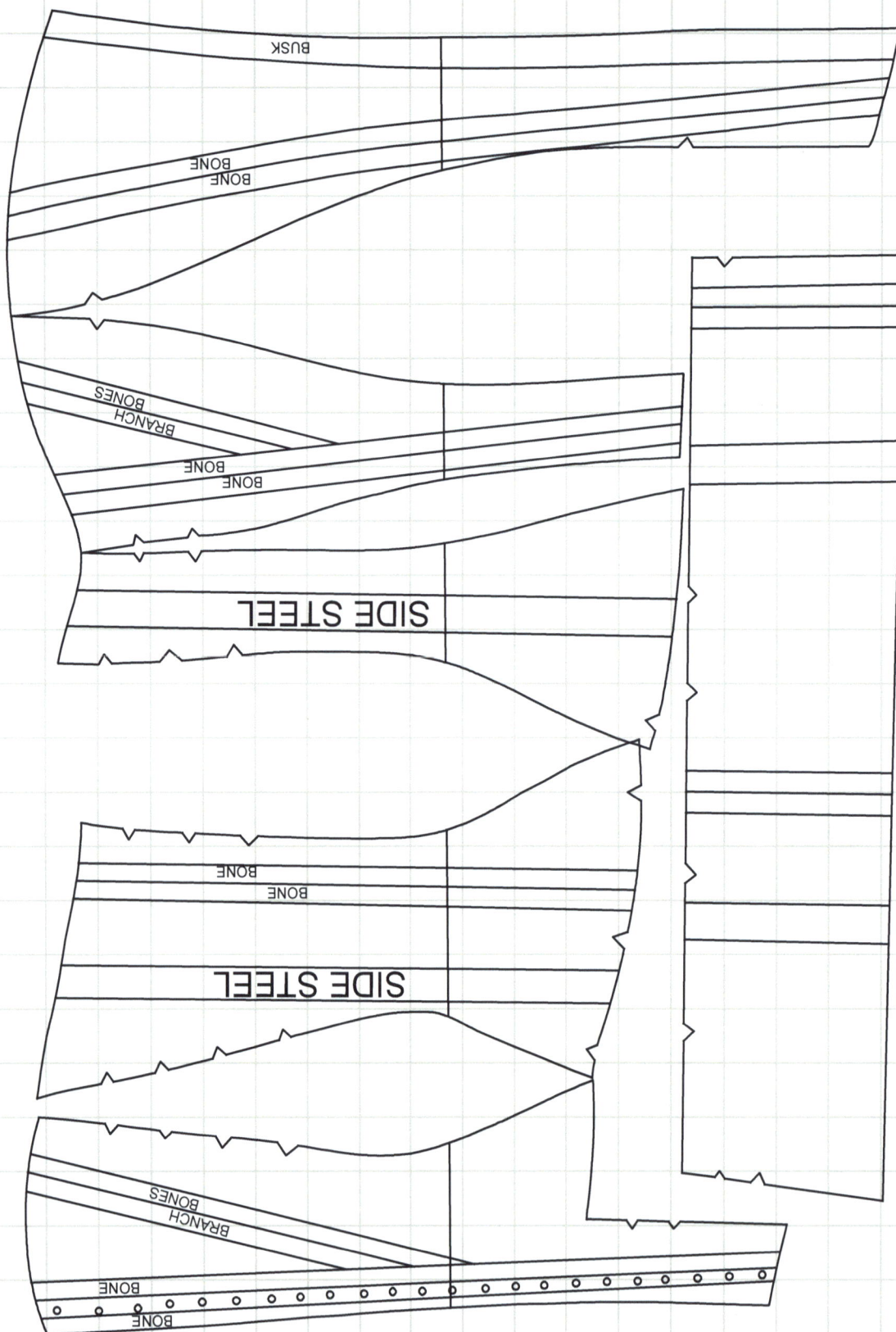

BUSK

BONE
BONE

BRANCH
BONES

BONE
BONE

SIDE STEEL

SIDE STEEL

BONE
BONE

BRANCH
BONES

BONE
BONE

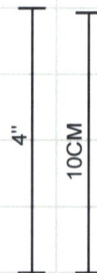

4"

10CM

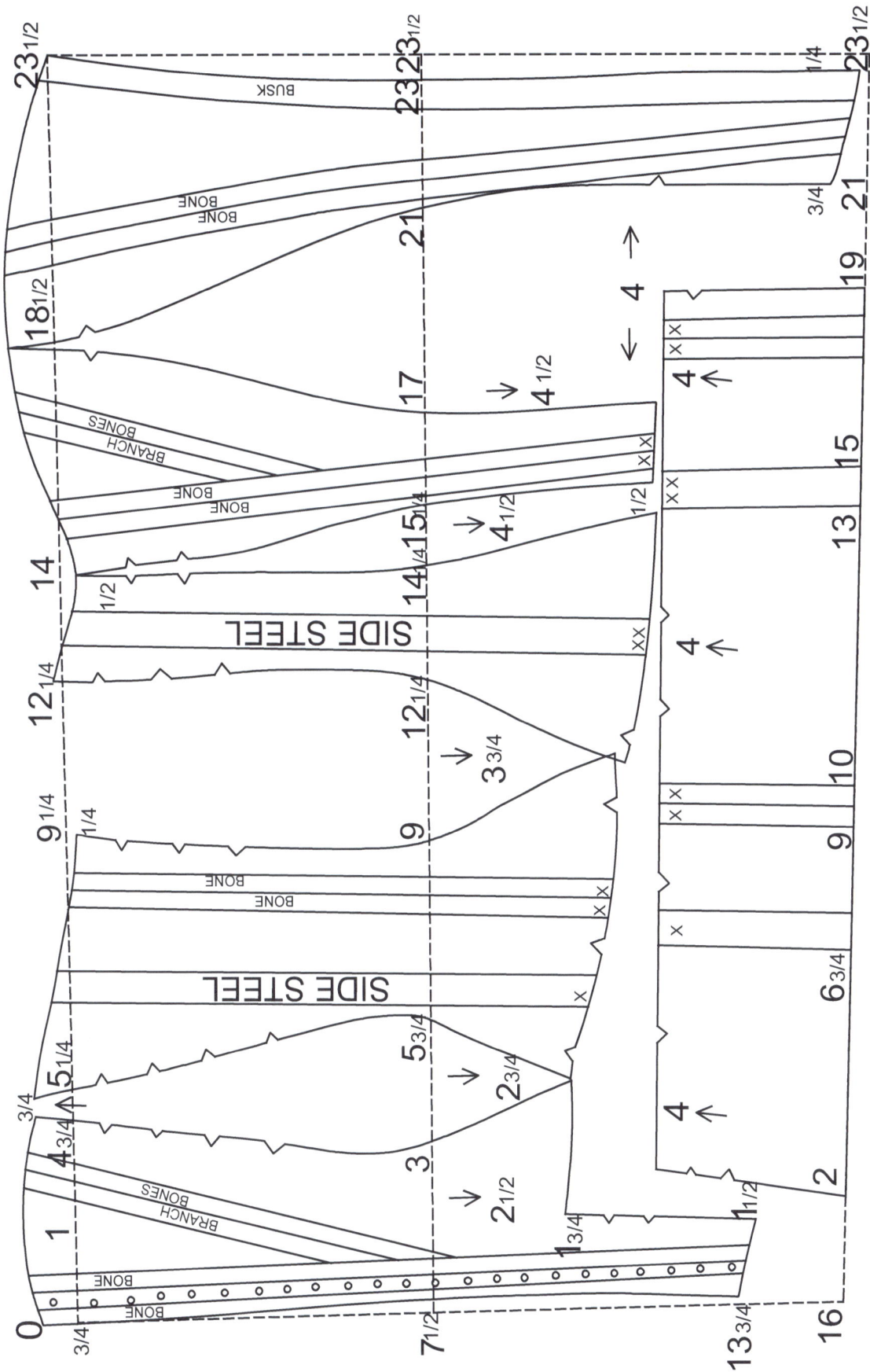

BUSK

BONE
BONE

BRANCH BONES

BONE

SIDE STEEL

SIDE STEEL

BONE
BONE

BRANCH BONES

BONE
BONE

0
3/4
3/4
4 3/4
5 1/4
1
9 1/4
1/4
12 1/4
14
1/2
18 1/2
23 1/2

7 1/2
2 1/2
3
5 3/4
2 3/4
9
3 3/4
12 1/4
14 15 1/4
4 1/2
17
4 1/2
21
23 23 1/2

1 3/4
1 1/2
2
6 3/4
9
10
13
15
19
21
23 1/2
1/4
3/4

13 3/4
16

4
4
4
4
4

x
x x
x x
x x
x x
x x
x x
1/2
1/2

4 ←
→ 4

4"
10CM

THELMA

LOW CUT CORSET 1911-1912

This is a low cut corset, with all round top, and cut in five pieces or sections for each half corset. It will be observed it is well hollowed out over the thighs, and it is an ideal corset for those who indulge in out-door sports and past-times as there is no restriction of movement when physical exercises are performed.

This corset with its medium bust line, and very distinctively cut lower edge dates to 1911-12. The height of the corset above the waist dropped in the early 1910s, from a full supportive bust, to a medium height bust, or lower. The different bust height measurements were helpfully defined by a corset designer in 1915:

"High bust, 6 to 7 1/2 inches; Medium bust, 4 1/2 to 5 1/2 inches; Low bust, 2 1/2 to 4 inches; Top less, 1 1/2 to 2 inches"[39]

The top of the corset is of a fashionable height for late 1911, early 1912, as described by Dry Goods Economist in December 1911:

"The average corset now takes care of the hips and waistline and has a top low enough to catch the curve of the bust and allow the figure to settle into the corset when in a sitting position. In other words the top of the new corset will adjust itself to almost any figure, the real corseting of the bust being left to the brassiere."

ON PREVOUS PAGES: THELMA
ROSEBUD COUTIL IN PINK FROM VENA CAVA DESIGN
LACE FROM LACEBEAUTY ON ETSY
CORSET CONSTRUCTED BY NIKKI SWIFT, NARROWED VISIONS CORSETS
MODEL, MAKE UP, HAIR AND PHOTOGRAPHY: ALIVYA V FREE

"The medium bust style is the big seller, the model for general distribution, and is featured for stout and medium, as well as slender figures. This line reaches the bust, but has curve enough to prevent the flesh from pushing up when the position of the wearer is changed."[40]

This corset is quite long over the hips, 15" from waist to lower edge over the hip. The Sears' 1912 catalog had two models noted as having an extreme length, "Ruth" at 14" and "Juanita" at 16".

Corsets with a similar shaped cut, but a much shorter skirt length over the hips, were also seen in 1915, 1916, 1918 and 1920.

18H151 Ruth 93c
Girdle top extra long hip corset for slender to medium figures. Made of a smooth finish Sterling cloth, a beautiful material of splendid wearing quality, with trimming of wide ribbon drawn lace. Four "double life" hose supporters, 1 1/4" wide. Non-rusting stays and clasps throughout. Length of front clasp, 10 1/2 inches; back steels, 14 1/2 inches. Extreme length over hips from waist line to bottom of skirt, 14 inches. Sizes 18 to 30. Shipping weight, 20 ounces
Sears Catalog, 1912(US)

18H230 Juanita $1.45
Medium bust, extreme long corset of elegant design, finish for all average sizes. Made of splendid quality good wearing coutil with eight good lisle elastic hose supporters 1 1/14 inches wide. Trimming of neat embroidery with satin ribbon bow and drawing cord to tighten top of bust. Front clasp, 12 inches long; back steels 14 1/2 inches long. Length from waist to bottom of skirt at hips, 16 inches. All non-rustable pliable boning. Sizes 18 to 30. Shipping weight 25 ounces. Sears Catalog, 1912 (US)

"National" Guaranteed Girdle-top "Free-Hip" Corset - a new sports model designed for misses and women of slender figure. For athletics, dancing or general wear. The material is good quality Brocade, and elastic webbing at sides of top provides comfortable expansion, while unboned hip sections leave the hips free. Shaped-out fronts. Flexible non-rustable boning. Four hose supporters. 8 1/2 inch front steels with hook below. Entire length of sides 14 inches. Colors white or pink. $1.29 White Coutil 96 c
National Cloak and Suit Spring-Summer 1918 (US)

375 Series General Utility Corset
Back-laced. Boned with Spirella. Straight clasp. Tape re-inforcement on inner side at bottom of clasp. Soft extension below clasp, hook and eye fastening. Shaped skirt. Unboned hip space. One set of hose supporters. Waist tape. Draw-tape. Trimmed according to material.
Standard sizes 20-30
Total front length: 12
Total side length 15"
Total back length: 15"
Spirella Catalog, 1920 (US)

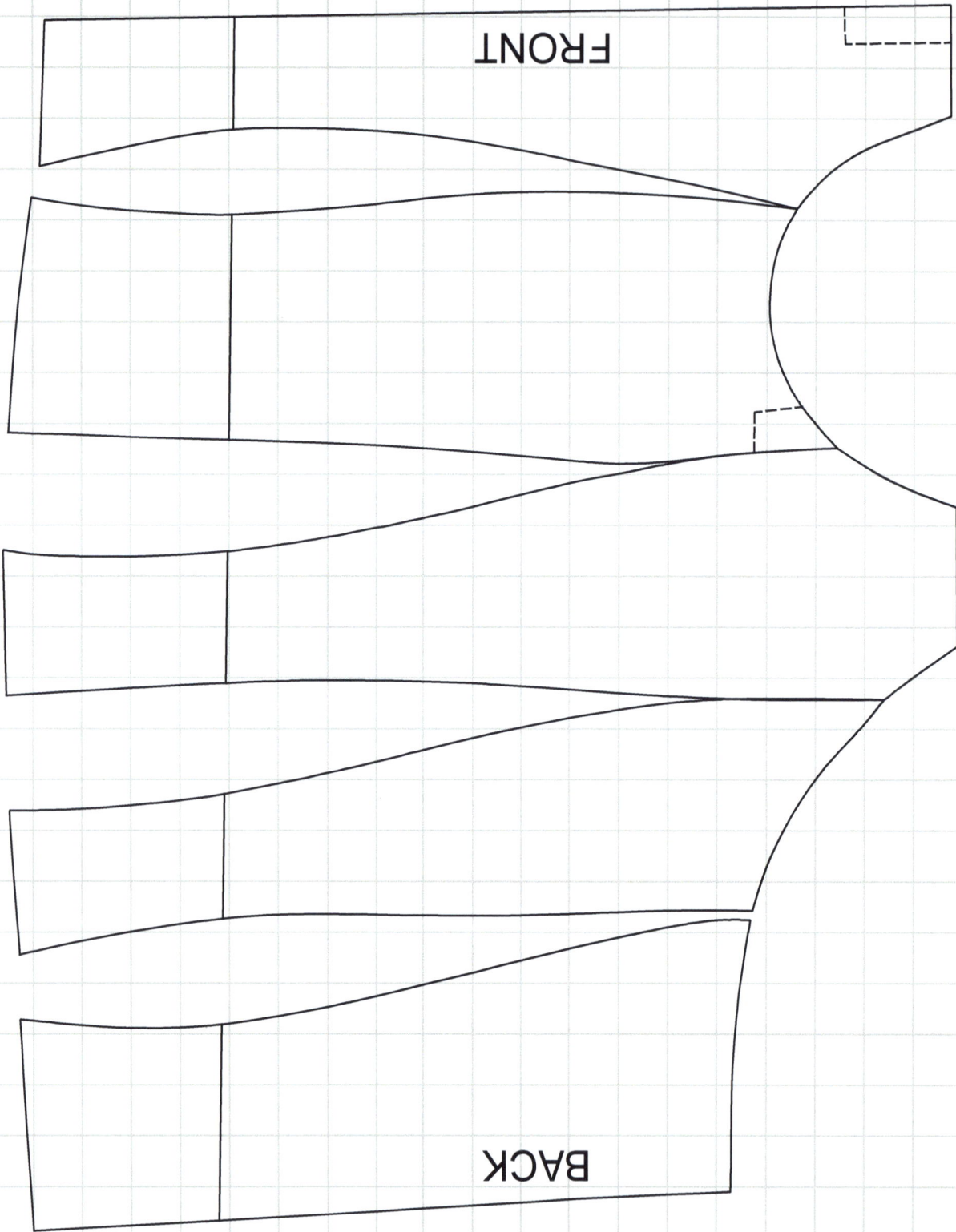

FRONT

BACK

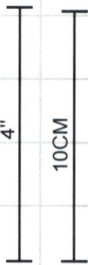

4"

10CM

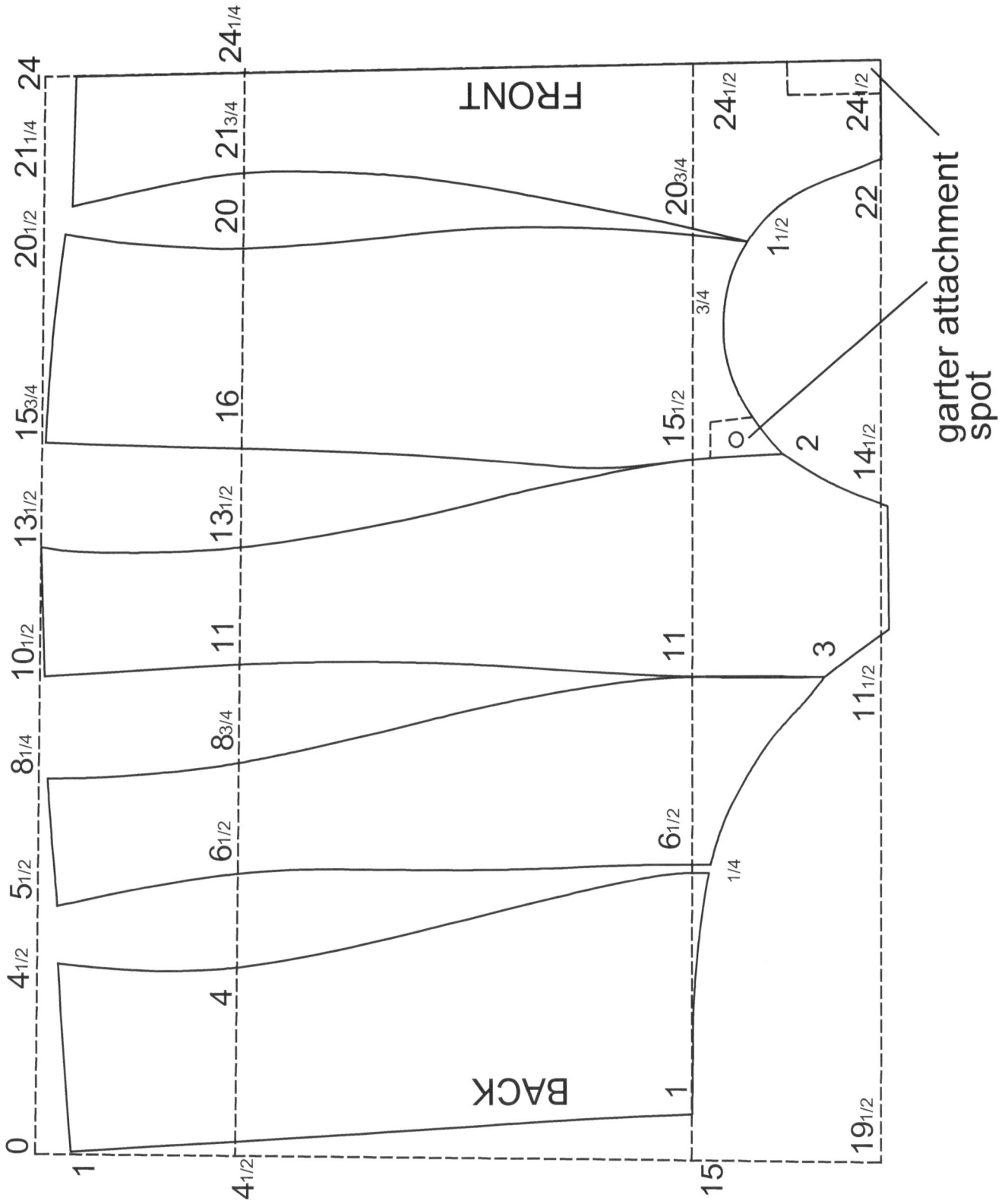

FRONT

BACK

garter attachment spot

24   24¼
21¼   21¾
20½   20
15¾   16
13½   13½
10½   11
8¼   8¾
5½   6½
4½   4
0

24½
24½
20¾
1½
3/4
15½
22
14½
2
11
3
11½
6½
1/4
19½
15
4½
1

4"
10CM

CORSET COVER
BRASSIERE 1905-1913

We have pleasure in placing before our readers the reduced model of a corset cover, which will be found very useful to ladies who are constantly wearing blouses. It is cut on the principle of a bodice, and is therefore fitted to the figure; it is boned with whalebone at the front in such a way that the bones may be removed for washing purposes.

The wearing of corset covers prevents dark corsets being seen through light blouses. Sometimes they are made from coloured muslins, but, as a general rule, white is mostly used. When cutting from the material, the front and the back parts are both put on the straight edge, so that the bias comes at the side seams.

In making-up, the seams are sown together in the ordinary way, and then top-stitched. Bone cases are marked on the pattern. Eyelet holes are put in the front to enable it to be fastened down on to the corset. Add strings, one of which passes through the buttonhole and ties in front. The top of the back is fastened with ordinary button and hole.

For young girls who participate in gymnastic and other exercises, this will be found an excellent substitute for corsets, especially when made from a little thicker material. This model will produce a garment suitable for a figure 40 breast, and 24 waist. There is no provision made for the seams.

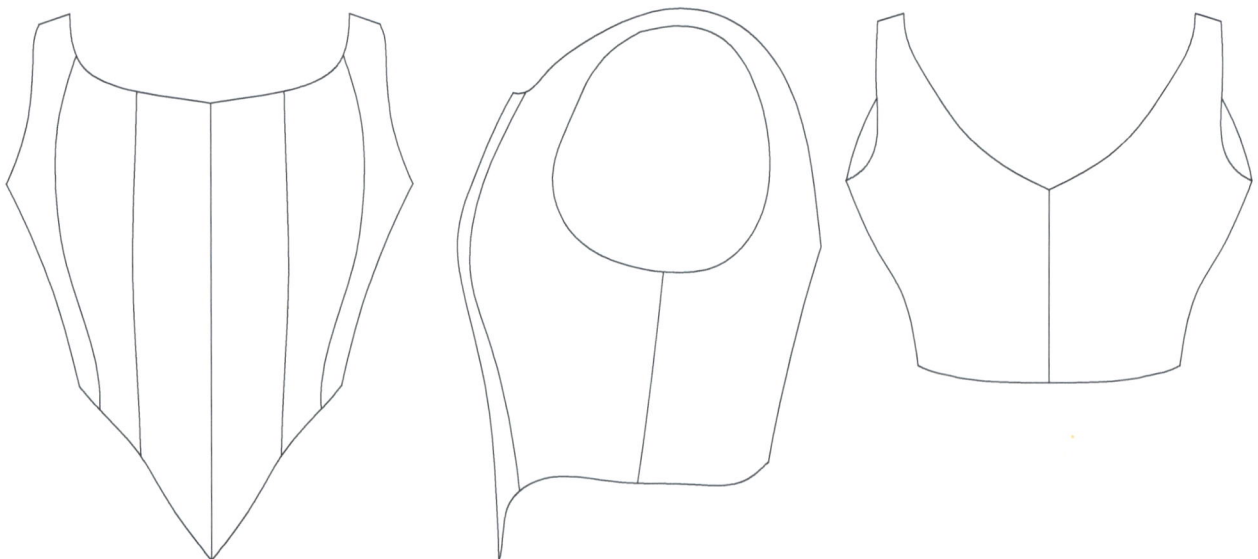

This Corset cover-brassiere most probably dates to around 1913, but could be from as early as 1905, there are similar styles available in catalogs from both of those years. As the bust level of the corset dropped to a lower level, and thus was not very supportive to the bust, it became necessary for women to wear something for support.

"The more general use of the low bust corset will bring forward more strongly than ever the claims of the brassiere, both as a separate article and in combination with the knickerbocker. New designs in brassieres, boned and unboned, are appearing in fall lines. Much development is expected in these accessories."

August 28, 1909 Dry Goods Economist, v.63 p.11[41]

The long pointed bodice is an unusual feature, as most brassieres during this time span, and later, were either cut straight across the front, or had a very short point, with a tape attached to the front which had a metal clip which attached to the corset clasps to prevent it from shifting. This pattern has a similar closure system to the 1913 Spirella brassiere seen below.

A 367 BRASSIERE, OF FINE WHITE CAMBRIC OR OF BLACK LAWN, TRIMMED WITH LACE AND RIBBON; SIZES 32 TO 46 INCH BUST, IN MEDIUM OR LONG WAIST. 98 CENTS
MACY'S FALL-WINTER 1905-06 CATALOG (US)

SPIRELLA BRASSIERE. STYLE 113 IS DESIGNED TO BE USED AS A CORSET COVER, HAVING SLIGHT CONFINING FEATURES. MADE ONLY IN RIVAL BATISTE, SUITABLY TRIMMED. HAS SPIRELLA BONING IN FRONT. CLOSES IN THE BACK WITH A BUTTON AND TAPE LOOP. REINFORCEMENT UNDER ARMS TO PROTECT THE GARMENT AT POINT OF WEAR. THESE GARMENTS ARE MADE LONG ENOUGH IN FRONT TO SLIP UNDER THE SKIRT BAND, PREVENTING THE SKIRT FROM SOILING CORSET; COMES ABOUT TO THE WAIST LINE IN THE BACK. THE BACK IS ADJUSTED BY MEANS OF A BUTTON AT THE TOP AND CONTROLLED AT THE BOTTOM BY TAPES WHICH PASS AROUND THE BODY AND TIE IN THE FRONT.
SPIRELLA'S 1913 ACCESSORIES CATALOG (US)

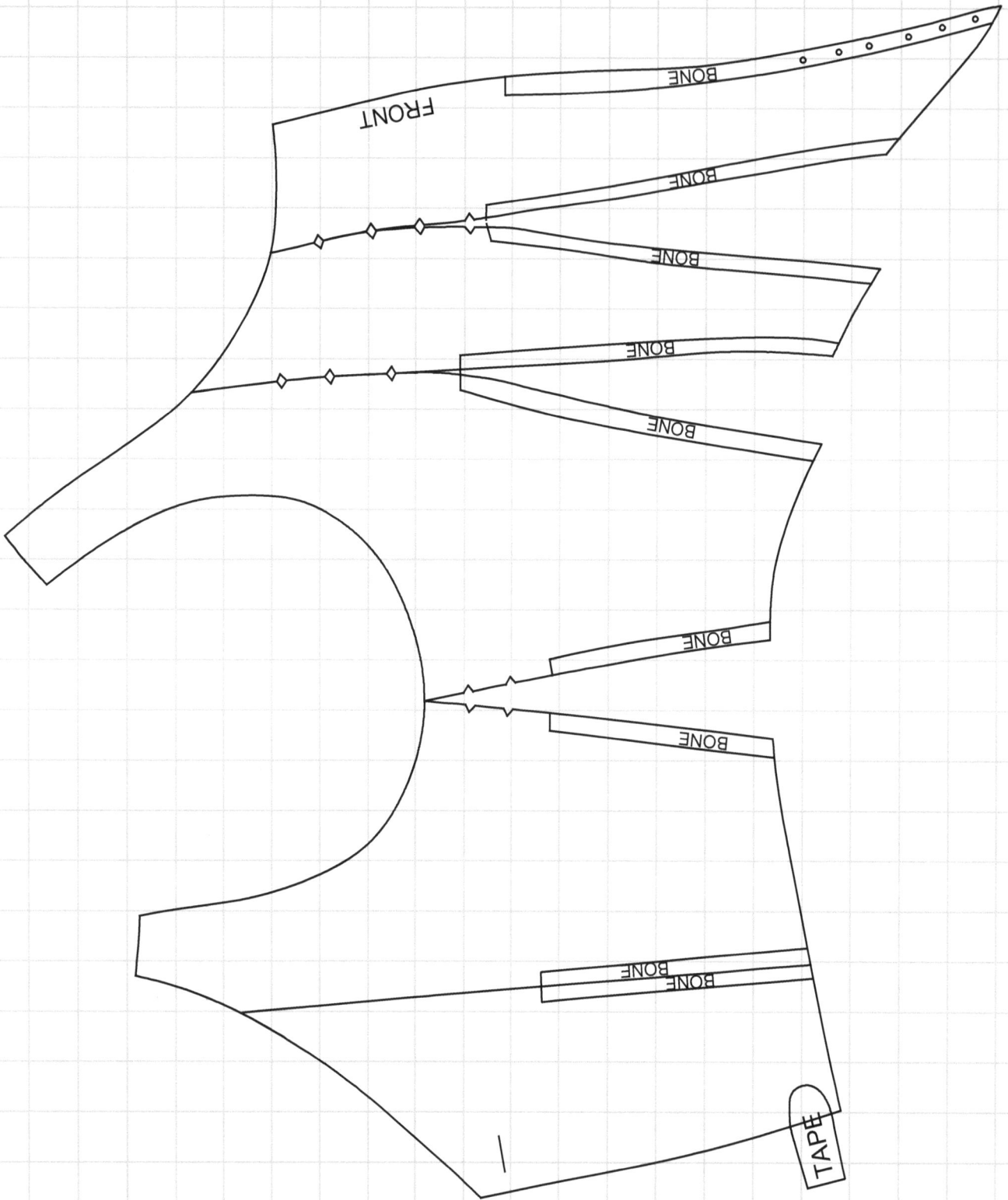

FRONT

BONE

BONE

BONE

BONE

BONE

BONE

BONE

BONE

BONE

TAPE

4"

10CM

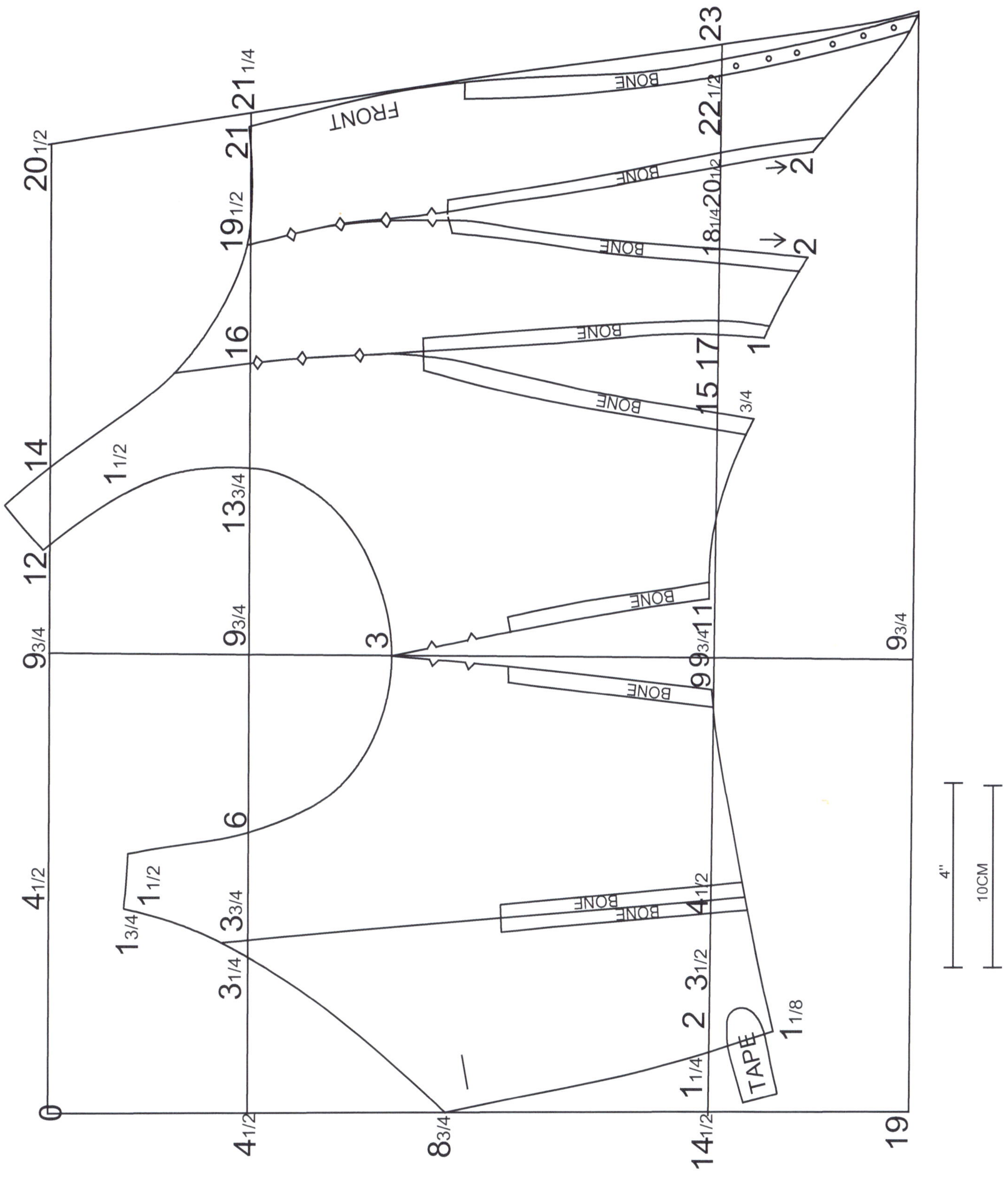

$20\tfrac{1}{2}$ $21\tfrac{1}{4}$ 23

BONE

FRONT

21 $22\tfrac{1}{2}$

$19\tfrac{1}{2}$ $18\tfrac{1}{4}$ $20\tfrac{1}{2}$

BONE → 2

BONE → 2

16

BONE

15 17 1

BONE

14 $\tfrac{3}{4}$

$1\tfrac{1}{2}$

12

$13\tfrac{3}{4}$

BONE

$9\tfrac{3}{4}$ $9\tfrac{3}{4}$

$9\tfrac{3}{4}$ 3

BONE

$9\,9\tfrac{3}{4}$ 11

$9\tfrac{3}{4}$

6

$4\tfrac{1}{2}$

$1\tfrac{3}{4}$ $1\tfrac{1}{2}$

$3\tfrac{3}{4}$

BONE

$3\tfrac{1}{4}$

BONE

$4\tfrac{1}{2}$

$3\tfrac{1}{2}$

2

$1\tfrac{1}{4}$

$1\tfrac{1}{8}$

TAPE

0

$4\tfrac{1}{2}$

$8\tfrac{3}{4}$

$14\tfrac{1}{2}$

19

4"

10CM

MARY

The large number of women employed in factories and works where the rigid rule enforced is that nothing in their apparel should contain any metallic substance whereby lives might be endangered, puts the ordinary corset, with its steel busks and stiffeners, metal eyelets, etc,, outside the region of desirable garments, where safety is of so much importance.

The corset here described has been designed to overcome all the objections which can be used against corsets generally of the types in vogue, by having nothing in its construction of a dangerous character.

Fashioned on hygienic lines, and constructed throughout of non-conductive materials, it forms an ideal corset for the factory worker who otherwise might have to do her work corsetless. Being a short corset it is advisable to use a good quality material, as the work in many cases is heavy, and the strain on the garment severe.

It will be seen that there are only four sections to each half of the corset, the seams being so arranged that the stiffeners, when placed under them, will be found to give ample support to the body, and prevent the garment from becoming wrinkled when worn. Light stripes of whalebone should be used for the stiffeners, as this is much stronger and more flexible than "Rio" [an imitation whalebone].

The buttonhole piece down the front is made from two strips of the material, 13 1/2 inches long by 2 inches wide, Turn over the edges 1/4 inch, and place the strips together, folded parts inside. Stitch along each edge and make another row of stitching down the middle to stiffen it. The sewn strip is then cut into nine pieces 1 1/2 inches long. This will make eight full pieces, and one for dividing into the smaller pieces at the top and bottom. The pieces are then joined on to one front section so

that the sewn edges meet closely together and form buttonholes. Strapping is then sewn along the seam to cover all raw edges, and the cut edges at the front neatly bound.

The button-piece is cut 12 inches long and 2 1/2 inches wide, folded down the centre and stitched close to the fold, and again 1/2 inch from it, to form a pocket for the stiffening. It is then joined to the other front section, and strapping sewn over the seam. Three pockets have thus been made for stiffening down the front, and ample support is obtained by them if good whalebone is used for the purpose.

In place of eyelets down the back, holes are pierced with a stiletto and worked by button hole stitching. The corset is laced and adjusted in the ordinary way.

Two-hole bone buttons strongly sewn on, are used with this kind of corset.

Many other women will find this type of corset equally suitable for them, and where their work is not of a dangerous kind, steels, eyelets, etc., can be used in place of whalebone.

Trimmed with lace, ribbon or embroidery, this corset makes a dainty and comfortable garment.

At the beginning of WWI, women flocked to fill the jobs left behind by the men heading to the front. Munitions making was one of the key war industries which hired women in record numbers. Munitions factories were afraid of sparks, and so banned all metal from clothing, including the metal bones inside of corsets How a metal bone inside of fabric, underneath more fabric of the outer clothes, could cause a spark is unknown.

This corset was designed to meet the munitions factory requirements of no metal bones, and has more in common with a corset waist as it has no busk, but fastens with buttons. The instructions for making up this corset are very similar to those of the children's waists.

American factories do not appear to have been as strict as English ones in their non-metal stance, as this American advertisement shows a metal busk on a war corset designed for munitions workers. However American factories did encourage women to work without corsets, as an American lady doctor complained about male physicians who thought that women could suddenly do strenuous work without injury, and stated that she felt that women needed the comfort and abdominal support of a good corset.[42]

M&P WAR CORSETS FOR WOMEN WORKERS YIELDS TO EVERY MOTION. ENTIRE TOPS OF ELASTIC. BONED FOR "FREE HIP" AND TO ALLOW UTMOST EASE WELL MADE FROM STRONG MATERIALS STYLE NO. 359 WHITE $10.00 PER DOZ., NO.360 PINK - $10.00 SIZES MADE - 19 TO 30 DERBY CORSET COMPANY THE CORSET AND UNDERWEAR REVIEW. V. 11 APRIL 1918, P.77

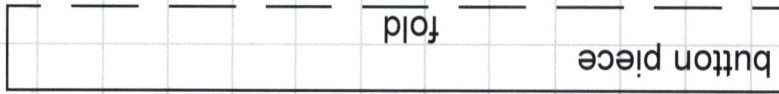

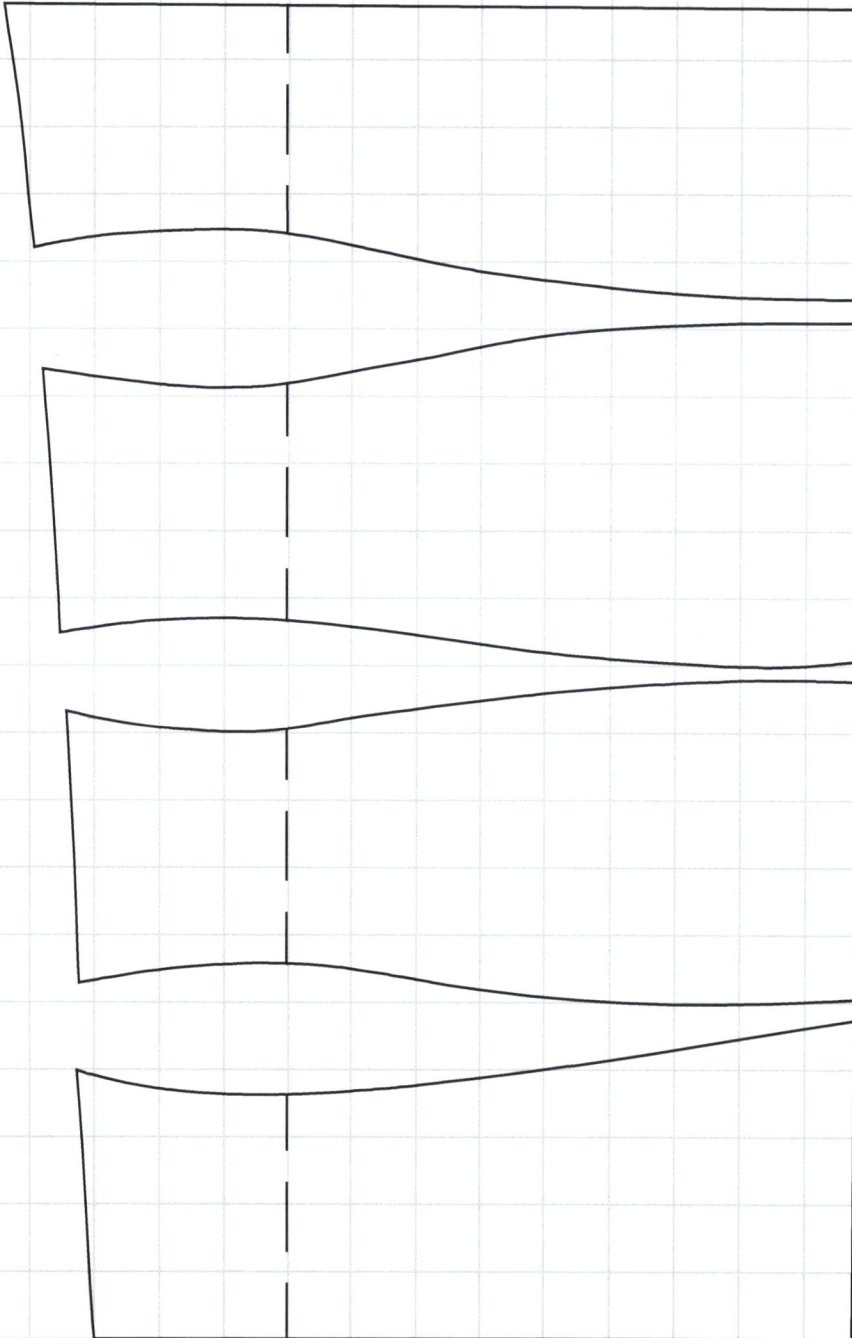

BACK

FRONT

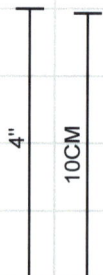

4"

10CM

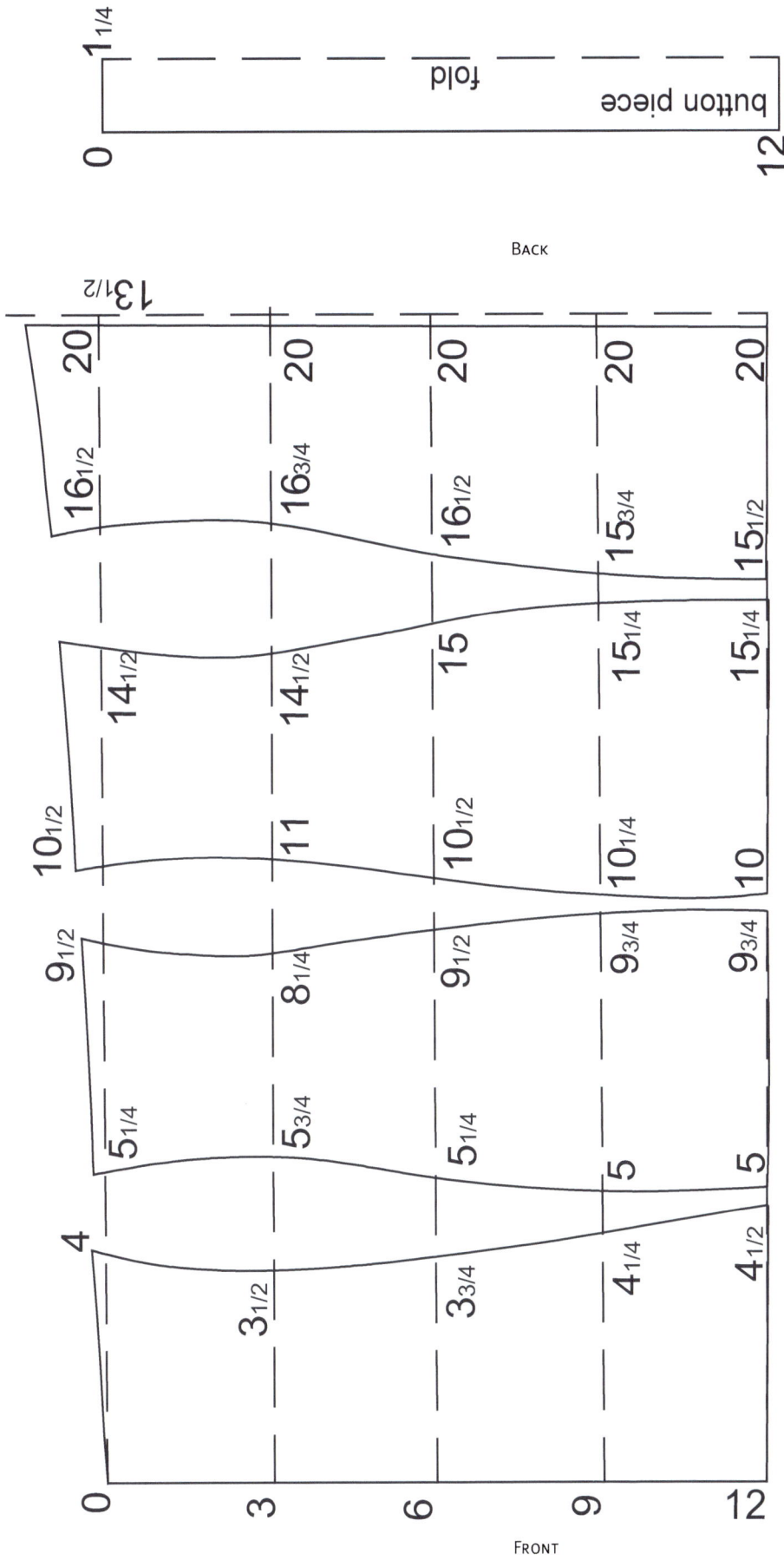

button piece

fold

1 1/4

0

12

BACK

13 1/2

20   20   20   20   20

16 1/2   16 3/4   16 1/2   15 3/4   15 1/2

14 1/2   14 1/2   15   15 1/4   15 1/4

10 1/2   11   10 1/2   10 1/4   10

9 1/2   8 1/4   9 1/2   9 3/4   9 3/4

5 1/4   5 3/4   5 1/4   5   5

4   3 1/2   3 3/4   4 1/4   4 1/2

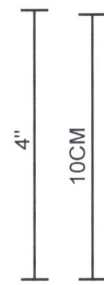

4"

10CM

0   3   6   9   12

FRONT

LILLIAN

FASHIONABLE CORSET 1916-1918

The set of patterns such as the diagram given on the next page forms one of the most fashionable corsets in use at the present day, and will be found to be all that an average figure could desire. Being exceedingly comfortable and well proportioned, yet fitting snugly and closely around the body, without any undue pressure on any portion of it, it moulds the figure into graceful lines, and gives the necessary support without any risk of harmful results.

If a diagram is reproduced by the ordinary inch tape it will give a pattern for a woman of average height and figure, with 22-inch waist, but with slight alterations can be adapted for either a tall or short person by increasing or diminishing the length of pattern as desired.

As the patterns are they produce a corset with waist line 3 1/2 inches from the top, 1/4 inch turnings being allowed on both sides of all sections. The sections are numbered 1, 2, 3, 4, 5, and 6, in consecutive order for making up, No. 1 on the left of the diagram being the front or busk piece, and No. 6 the back.

ON PREVIOUS PAGES: LILLIAN
SPOT BROCHE, IN CREAM AND PINK FROM VENA CAVA DESIGN
LACE FROM LACEBEAUTY ON ETSY
CORSET CONSTRUCTED BY NIKKI SWIFT, NARROWED VISIONS CORSETS
MODEL, MAKE UP, HAIR AND PHOTOGRAPHY: ALIVYA V FREE

In 1915 and early 1916, the corset fashions had favored a longer skirt, to better control the hips and thighs. But in late 1916, the skirt of the corset shortened, and would remain shorter through the 1920s. This fashionable corset dates to 1916-1918, with it's medium height bust and hip, natural lines to the waist, and curving lower edge. The Delineator magazine described latest corset fashions in 1917:

"The present silhouette is so perfect that until something better can be invented, it would be wicked to change it. The corset follows the natural lines of the figure indicating but not increasing the curve of the waist at the side, allowing the bust to fall into its natural place, keeping the hips and thighs as small as possible by means of a fairly long skirt, boned sufficiently to give support and control the abdomen, but with a moderate, reasonable amount of boning so that the figure appears soft and supple, and natural."[43]

74-1750 ACME CORSET
THE MOST SUITABLE MODEL FOR SLIGHT AND MEDIUM FIGURES. MADE OF GOOD QUALITY WHITE COUTIL, BONED WITH FINELY TEMPERED STEELS. MEDIUM BUST AND HIP. STRONG HOOK AND EYE IN THE SKIRT BELOW THE FRONT CLASP. FOUR HOSE SUPPORTERS. A COMFORTABLE, WELL-MADE, LIGHT-WEIGHT CORSET. SIZES 18 TO 26 INCHES. 50 CENTS
1916 EATONS CATALOG (CANADA)

98-A352
AN R&G MODEL, PARTICULARLY SUITABLE FOR THE SHORT AVERAGE FIGURE. MADE OF WHITE COUTIL. THE BUST IS CUT LOW TO ENSURE COMFORT AND IS TRIMMED WITH A FOLD OF BATISTE AND INSERTION. MEDIUM LONG HIP AND SKIRT. THE BONING IS RUSTLESS AND PLIABLE. FOUR HOSE SUPPORTERS OF GOOD QUALITY ELASTIC. SIZES 19 TO 28 PRICE $1.50
1917 EATONS CATALOG (CANADA)

FOR AVERAGE TO SLENDER FIGURES
NO. 18N135
TRULY COMFORTABLE LOW BUST MODEL, EXCEPTIONALLY POPULAR WITH YOUNG WOMEN. A VERY SPECIAL VALUE. SPLENDID WEARING STRONG GARMENT. MADE OF GOOD QUALITY COUTIL. PRETTY EMBROIDERY TRIMMING. FOUR GOOD HOSE SUPPORTERS. HEIGHT OF BUST, 3 1/2 INCHES ABOVE WAISTLINE. CLASP, 10 INCHES LONG WITH TWO STRONG HOOKS BELOW. SIZES, 19 TO 26. PRICE $1.48
SEARS CATALOG, 1918 (US)

Back

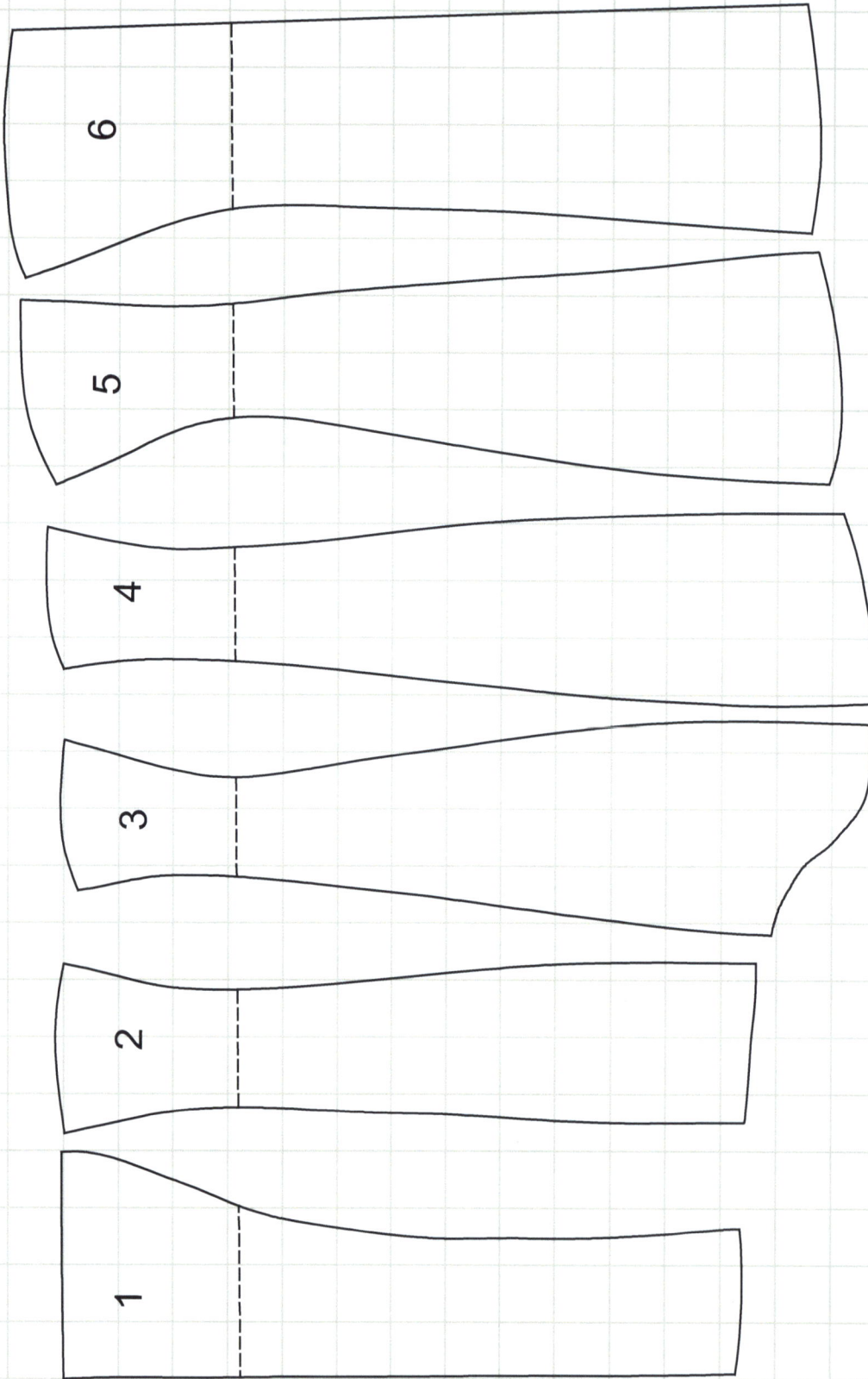

6

5

4

3

2

1

Front - Busk

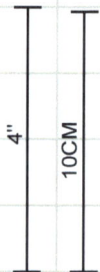

4"

10CM

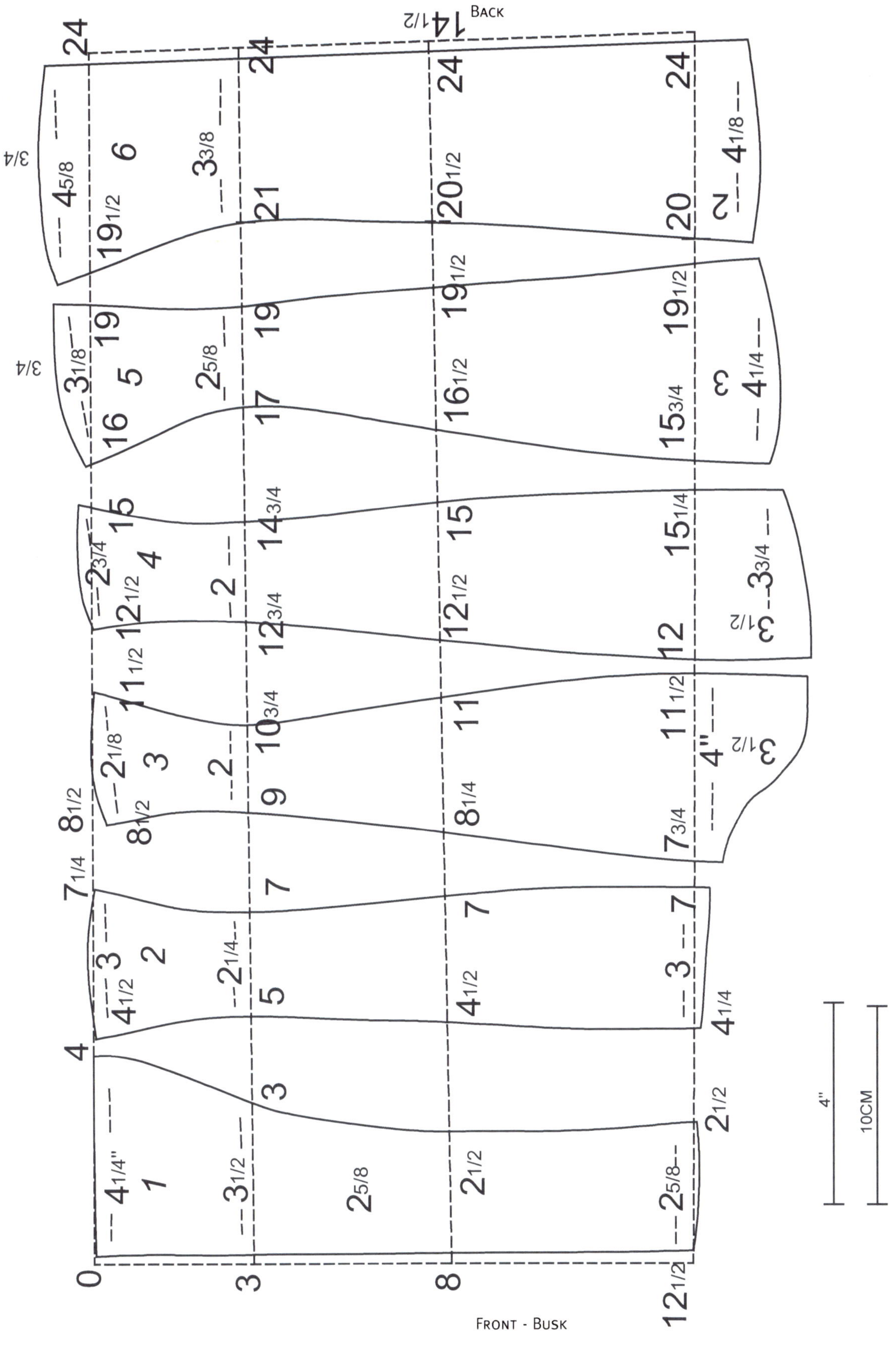

Back

Front - Busk

1/4 INCH SEAM ALLOWENCES ALLOWED ON ALL PIECES

4"

10CM

CLARA

STRAIGHT HIP CORSET 1916-1920

The first one illustrated is cut low, with an all round top, and has a straight hip. The advantage of the straight hip, cut medium length is that good support is given below the waist.

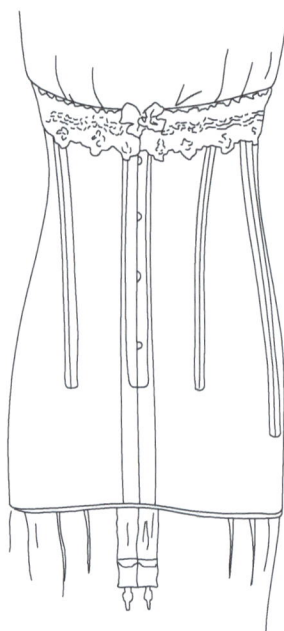

Clara and the next corset, Ruby, are very similar corsets, with some slight styling and sizing differences. Designed for stout figures, Clara has a waist of 35 inches, which is the largest waist of any of the corsets in the book. With it's low bust, medium hip corset dates to late 1916, to early 1917, and would have been at the cutting edge of fashion for Spring 1917:

New Spring Corsets

"A single glance does not reveal all the fine points, or rather lines, of the newest corsets. One sees that the figures are beautiful, but the reasons for that are many. In the first place the bust line is lower, as predicted in the October Review. It is placed in the majority of cases from two to three inches above the waist, perhaps slightly higher in the back. This allows more of the natural lines of the figure and eliminates stiffness. [...] Below the waist, too, there is more curve than formerly. This brings out the waist more clearly and also allows elbow-room for the figure to retain its curves and not be pushed out of place by stiff, straight lines.

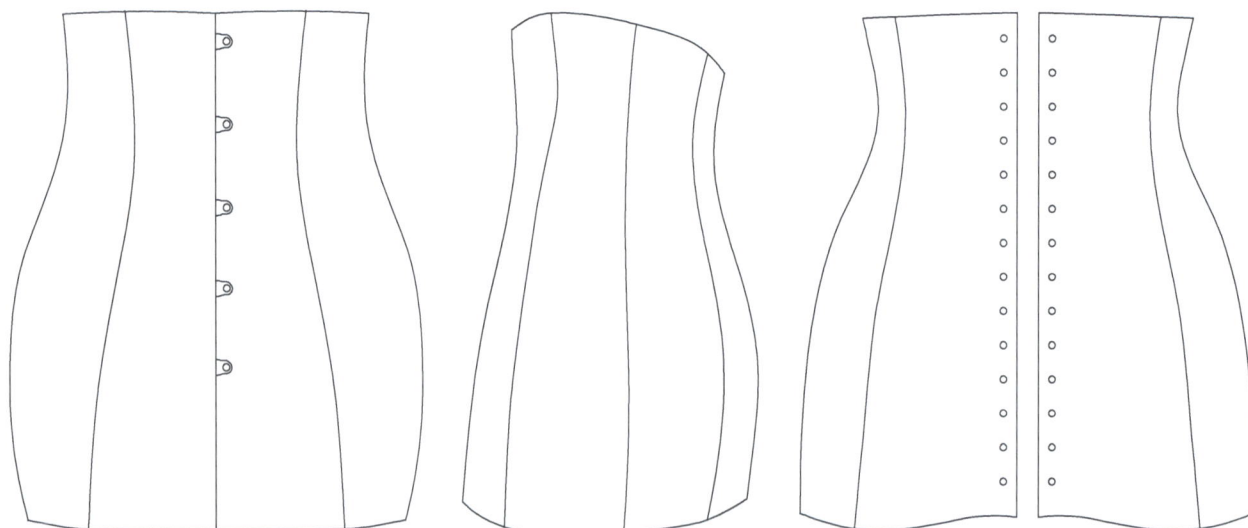

The natural sequence of this alteration is the shorter skirt to the corset. The longer skirt is no longer necessary to secure the figure. Now it is just long enough to follow the natural lines and retain them. There is less boning than formerly, and only for very stout figures is stiffening allowed over the hip-bones."[44]

Canadian Dry Goods Review, January 1917

Although the fashion prediction mentions less boning, the illustration and the catalog advertisements all show double bones on each seam. Corsets similar in style and bust height would continue to be sold into the early 1920s.

74-1753 A PARTICULARLY GRACEFUL AND COMFORTABLE CORSET, DESIGNED TO GIVE TO SLIGHT AND MEDIUM FIGURES THE NECESSARY SUPORT AND A GRACEFUL CONTOUR. MADE OF FINE QUALITY WHITE COUTIL, LOW BUST TRIMMED WITH LACE AND RIBBON. MEDIUM LONG HIP, WITH A TRIANGULAR GUSSET OF ELASTIC IN THE BACK (SEE SMALL INSET) WHICH TAKES CARE OF THE SURPLUS FLESH ACROSS THE HIPS AND PREVENTS THE CORSET EDGE FROM SHOWING THROUGH THE THINNEST GOWN.
SIZES 18 TO 28 INCHES. PRICE 1.25
1916 EATONS CATALOG (CANADA)

98-1528
THIS CORSET OF HANDSOME BROCADE HAS BEEN CONSTRUCTED ALONG THE LATEST FASHION LINES. IT GIVES THE SLIGHT INCURVE AT THE WAIST. LOW BUST, TRIMMED WITH DAINTY INSERTION, LONG HIP AND SKIRT. SIX HOSE SUPPORTERS OF GOOD QUALITY WEBBED ELASTIC. SUITABLE FOR AVERAGE FIGURES. SIZES 20-28. PRICE 2.50
1917 EATONS CATALOG (CANADA)

THE 667 SERIES -60 TYPE BACK-LACED. BONED WITH SPIRELLA. STRAIGHT CLASP. TAPE REINFORCEMENT ON INNER SIDE AT BOTTOM OF CLASP. SOFT EXTENSION BELOW CLASP, HOOK AND EYE FASTENING. SKIRT CUT STRAIGHT. ONE SET OF HOSE SUPPORTERS. WAIST TAPE. DRAW-TAPE. BONED TO AVOID PRESSURE OVER POINT OF HIP BONES. TRIMMED ACCORDING TO MATERIAL.
SPIRELLA 1920 CATALOG (US)

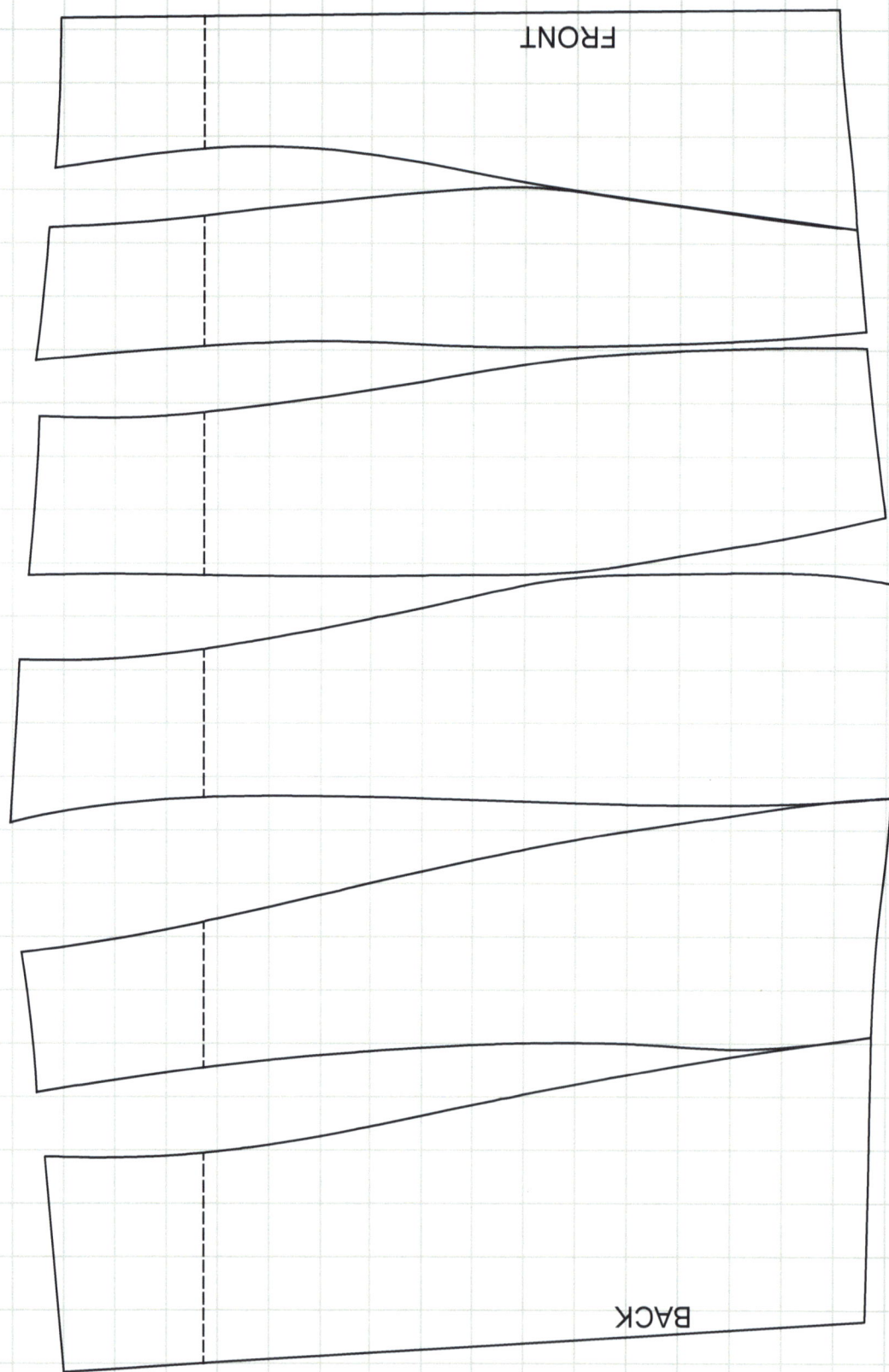

FRONT

BACK

4"

10CM

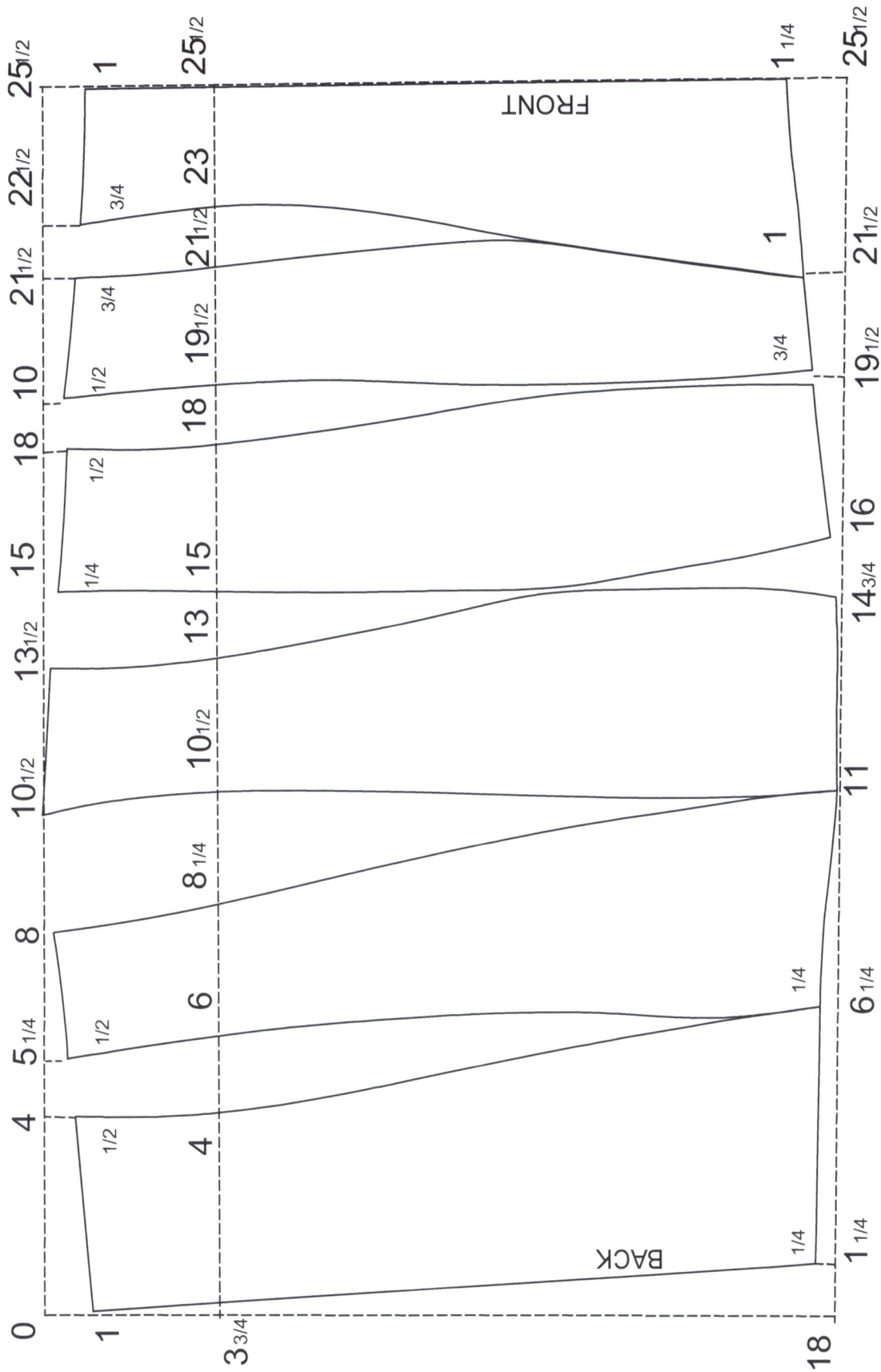

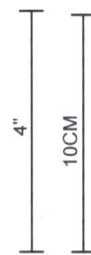

RUBY

ELASTIC LONG LINE CORSET 1917-1921

The other one has elastic inserted at the top, and is also cut low at the bust, whilst it is so fashioned that the ridge of flesh above the corset, so often the result of elastic, is entirely obviated. It also emphasises the long, straight hip line.

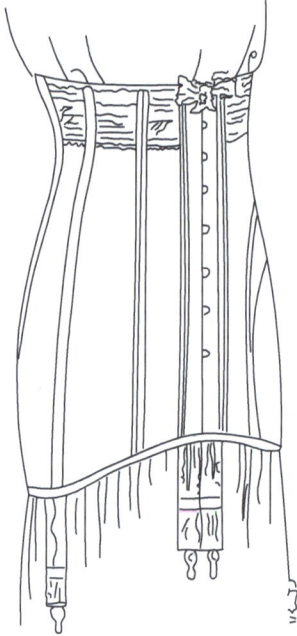

Although elastic was used earlier in athletic corsets, it was not a normal feature of a fashionable corset. But starting in 1915-1916, it began to be used as small gussets at the rear, and then as larger sections at the top. Beginning in 1917, larger sections of elastic were added to the tops of fashionable corsets to allow for freedom of movement.

"The fitting of the figure is being managed more and more deftly by means of rubber gores and inserts, which hold in the figure without making it hard and stiff. The top of many of the new corsets is low, in fact, scarcely a top at all. Of course many women cling to a higher top, especially if they have large figures, but for the slight figure or for a woman of average size, the top is decidedly low."[45]
Delineator, September 1917

This corset has a medium bust of 4 1/4 inches, in line with fashionable corsets for 1917, but higher than the catalog examples below. Similar corsets with minimal height above the waist are seen in catalogs through the end of the 1920s, but this particular bust height and skirt length, with an elastic top, would have been fashionable from 1917-1921.

98-1765 THIS ACME CORSET WILL BE APPRECIATED BY THE WOMAN WHO REQUIRES ONLY A MODERATE DEGREE OF SUPPORT AND DESIRES A COOL, COMFORTABLE MODEL FOR THE WARM WEATHER. IT IS ALSO A SPLENDID MODEL FOR DANCING OR ATHLETICS. THE MATERIAL USED IS WHITE COUTIL. THE EXTREMELY LOW BUST HAS AN INSET OF ELASTIC TO ALLOW PLENTY OF BREATHING SPACE. NOT ALSO THE INSET OF ELASTIC IN THE BACK, MEDIUM HIP, FOUR HOSE SUPPORTERS. SIZES 18 TO 28 PRICE 1.00
1917 SPRING AND SUMMER EATONS CATALOG (CANADA)

98-A200 THIS CORSET IS MADE OF HANDSOME PINK BROCADE, JUST BONED ENOUGH TO HOLD THE FIGURE SNUGLY, AND IS SUITABLE FOR ANY PURPOSE, WHERE FLEXIBILITY AND STYLE ARE FACTORS. THE LOW GIRDLE TOP HAS A WIDE SECTION OF FANCY ELASTIC ACROSS THE TWO SIDE SECTIONS, WHICH ALLOWS FOR PLENTY OF BREATHING SPACE AND FREEDOM OF MOVEMENT. MEDIUM LONG SKIRT. FOUR HOSE SUPPORTERS. SIZES 20 TO 26. PRICE 3.50
1917 SPRING AND SUMMER EATONS CATALOG (CANADA)

10F27 - A LOW-TOPPED CORSET ESPECIALLY DESIGNED FOR SLENDER TO MEDIUM FULL FIGURES. MADE OF WELL-WEARING MERCERIZED BROCADE. IT CONFINES THE THIGHS AND LOWER HIPS, GIVING A STRAIGHT LINE DOWN THE BACK, IN ACCORD WITH THE DICTATES OF THE LATEST MODE. THE ELASTIC WEBBING INSERTS ON TOP ASSURE EASE AND FREEDOM OF MOVEMENT. SLIGHTLY BONED WITH RUST-PROOF FLEXIBLE BONING, LONG SKIRT. TWO PAIRS OF GARTERS. COLORS: FLESH PINK OR WHITE. SIZES 20-30 INCHES. $1.79
1919-1920 FALL WINTER PERRY, DAME & CO. (US)

98-1318 ACME SLIGHT FIGURE MODEL SIZES 19 TO 26
A MOST COMFORTABLE ACME CORSET FOR SLIGHT AND MEDIUM FIGURES, WHO DESIRE PERFECT FREEDOM ABOVE THE WAISTLINE, AND A WELL CORSETED EFFECT BELOW. MADE A WHITE COUTIL WITH AN ELASTIC BAND AT THE WAISTLINE. MEDIUM HIP AND SKIRT, STRONG HOOK AND EYE BELOW FRONT CLASP. FOUR HOSE SUPPORTERS. PRICE 2.10
1920-1921 FALL AND WINTER EATONS CATALOG (CANADA)

98-1318

Front

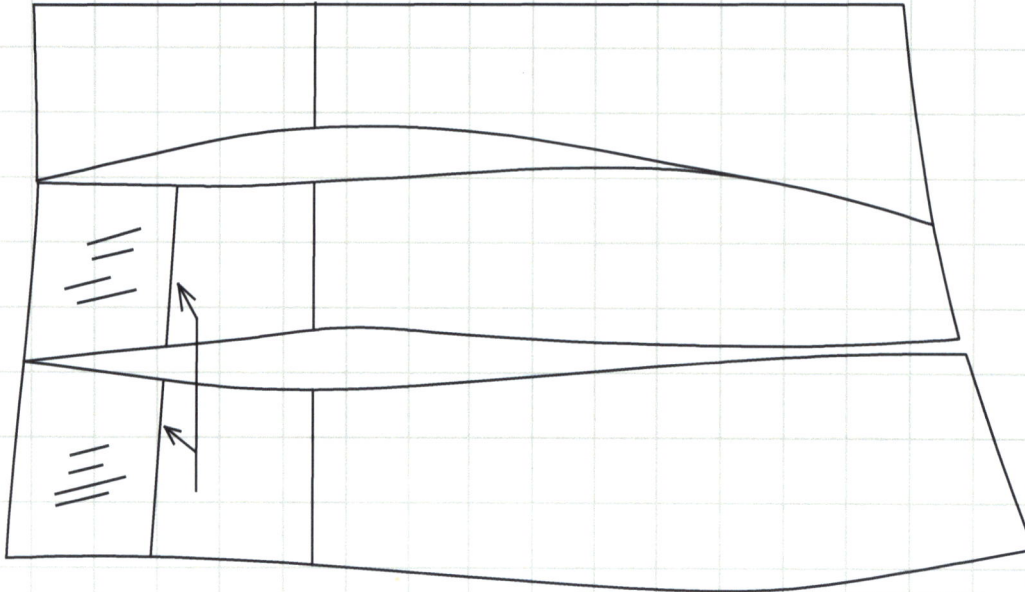

ELASTIC

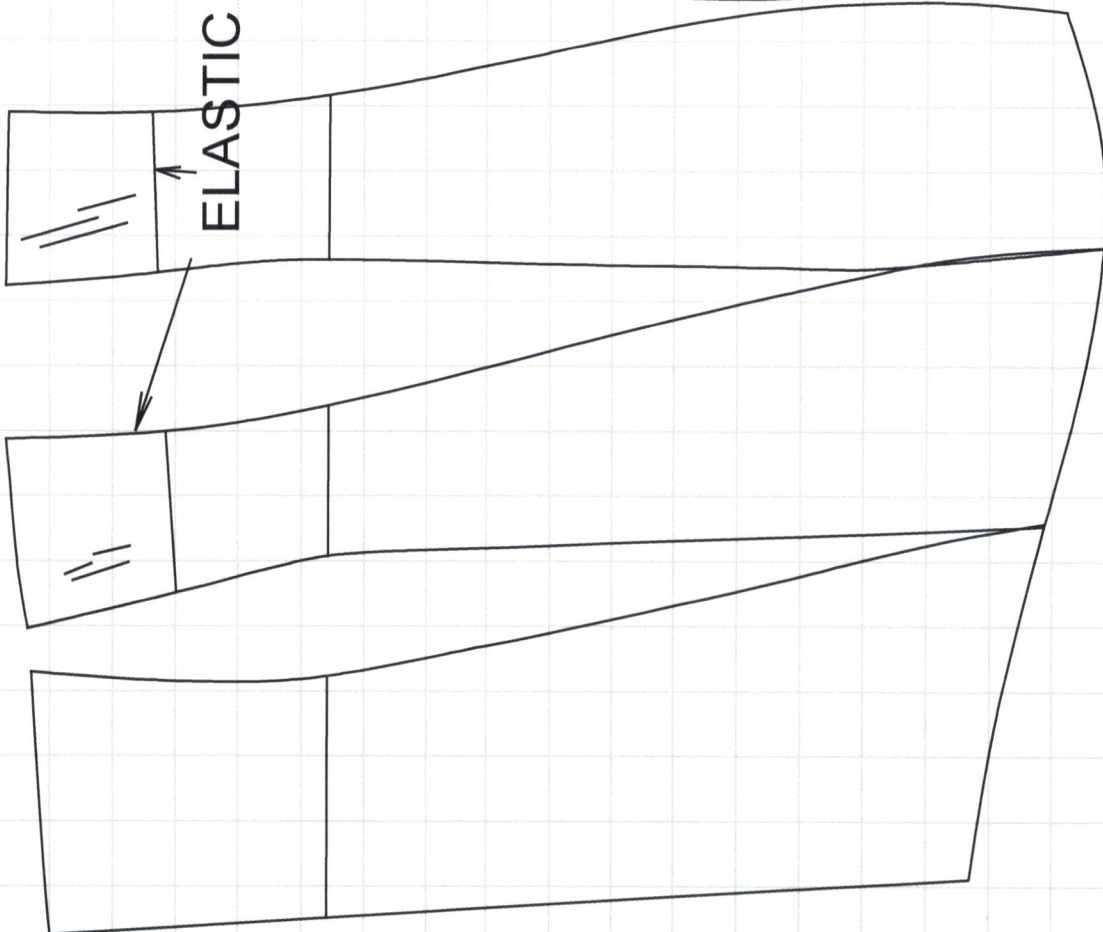

4"

10CM

Back

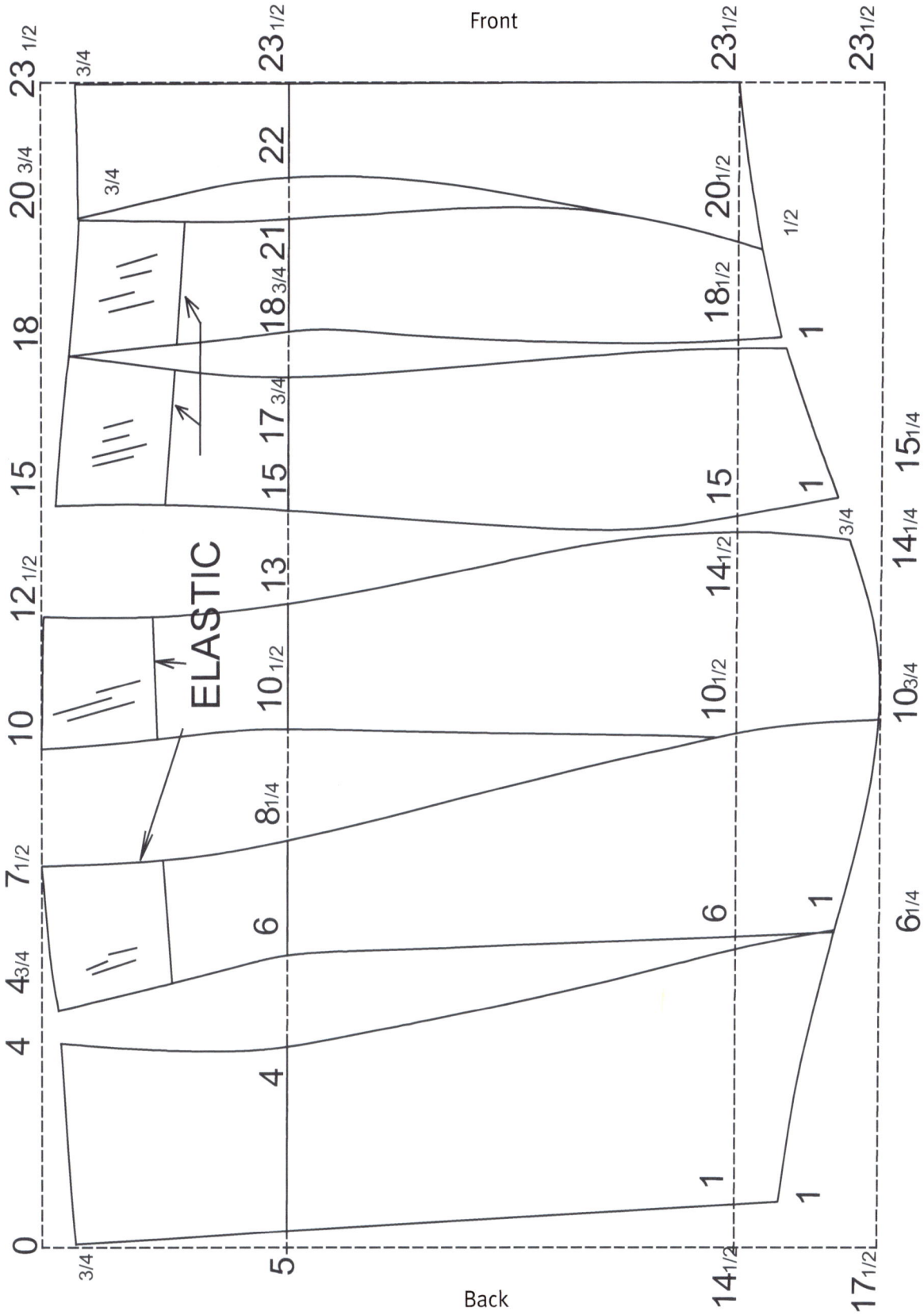

Front

Back

ELASTIC

23 ½   23 ½   23 ½   23 ½

3/4   3/4

22

20 3/4   20 ½   20

18   18 3/4 21   18 ½

15   17 3/4   15   15 ¼

1/2

1

1

12 ½   13

10   10 ½   10 ½   10 ¾

8 ¼   14 ½   14 ¼

7 ½   6   6   6 ¼

4 ¾   1   1

4   4   1

5

0   3/4   14 ½   17 ½

3/4

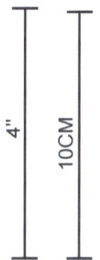

4"

10CM

MYRTLE

CORSET WITH HIP CONTROL BANDS 1918

The diagrams of this type of corset are self- explanatory. The upper portion is cut in six half sections, while the bottom portion is in three transverse sections, the object of which is to reduce the figure to the smallest possible proportions.

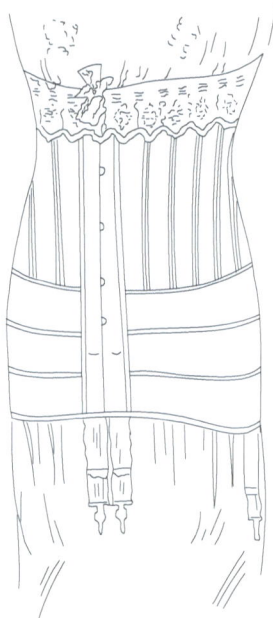

This corset with lower bands to control the hips is an unusual style, as this was not a common design for stout corsets in the late Teens. However, it does allow for very easy dating, as it is very similar in style to a corset advertised by R&G Corset Company as a new Spring model in April 1918.[46]

The illustration included with the pattern (left) includes a separate straight piece in the front for the busk, although the pattern diagram doesn't include it, and there is no mention of it in the very short text description. This separate busk piece would become a common design feature in the 1920s, but in the late Teens, this was only seen on about half of the corsets represented in catalogs.

ON PREVIOUS PAGES: MYRTLE
DIAMOND BROCHE IN NUDE FROM VENA CAVA DESIGN
LACE FROM LACEBEAUTY ON ETSY
CORSET CONSTRUCTED BY NIKKI SWIFT, NARROWED VISIONS CORSETS
MODEL, MAKE UP, HAIR AND PHOTOGRAPHY: ALIVYA V FREE
CORSET PHOTOGRAPHED BY NIKKI SWIFT

R&G CORSET MODEL E 530
(ON RIGHT)
DESIGNED FOR FULL FIGURES.
REINFORCED FRONT. LONG SKIRT.
WEDGE CLASP GIVES ADDED
STRENGTH. WHITE OR PINK
COUTIL.
MCCALL'S MAGAZINE FOR JUNE,
1918, P.56

Two typical stout corsets for 1918
2V929 FOR LARGE FIGURES
THIS "NATIONAL" GUARANTEED CORSET
IS A STRONG, SPLENDIDLY DESIGNED
MODEL THAT GIVES REMARKABLY
STYLISH LINES TO LARGE FIGURES. IT IS
HIGH ENOUGH IN THE BACK TO PREVENT
THE ROLL OF FLESH THAT IS APT TO
COME JUST UNDER THE SHOULDERS,
AND IN FRONT IT IS JUST THE CORRECT
HEIGHT TO HOLD THE FIGURE WITHOUT
RAISING THE BUST. NON-RUSTABLE
BONING, EXTRA SUPPORT AT THE SIDES,
GIVES PERFECT FIGURE SUPPORT, YET
IS SO FLEXIBLE IT YIELDS TO EVERY
MOVEMENT. BONING STITCHED IN
POCKETS TO PREVENT SLIPPING. LONG
SKIRT; GORED BUST. HEIGHT OF BUST
4 1/2 INCHES ABOVE WAISTLINE. 11-INCH
FRONT CLASP, WITH ELASTIC LACES
BELOW. SIX HOSE SUPPORTERS.
GOOD QUALITY WHITE COUTIL.
SIZES 24 TO 36. $2.98
1918 NATIONAL CLOAK & SUIT CATALOG
(US)

2V913 THIS "NATIONAL"
GUARANTEED CORSET HAS
BEEN ESPECIALLY DESIGNED TO
PROVIDE EASE AND COMFORT
FOR WOMEN OF MEDIUM TO FULL
FIGURES WITHOUT SACRIFICING
STYLE. IT IS ONE OF OUR MOST
POPULAR MODELS AND IS MADE
OF SPLENDID QUALITY COUTIL.
CUT LOW UNDER THE ARMS AND
MODERATELY HIGH IN THE BACK
TO SUPPORT THE FLESH. A WIDE
INSERT OF FINEST QUALITY ELASTIC
WEBBING EXTENDING FROM FRONT
TO SIDE-BACK STEELS REDUCES
PROMINENT ABDOMEN AND
CONTROLS LARGE HIPS WITHOUT
DISCOMFORT. VERY FLEXIBLE NON-
RUSTABLE ALUMINUM-FINISHED
BONING. FOUR DURABLE HOSE
SUPPORTERS. LOW BUST 3 1/2
INCHES ABOVE WAIST-LINE. FRONT
CLASP 10 1/2 INCHES LONG WITH
FIVE STRONG HOOKS BELOW.
WHITE ONLY. SIZES: 20 TO 36.
$2.49
1918 NATIONAL CLOAK & SUIT
CATALOG (US)

Front

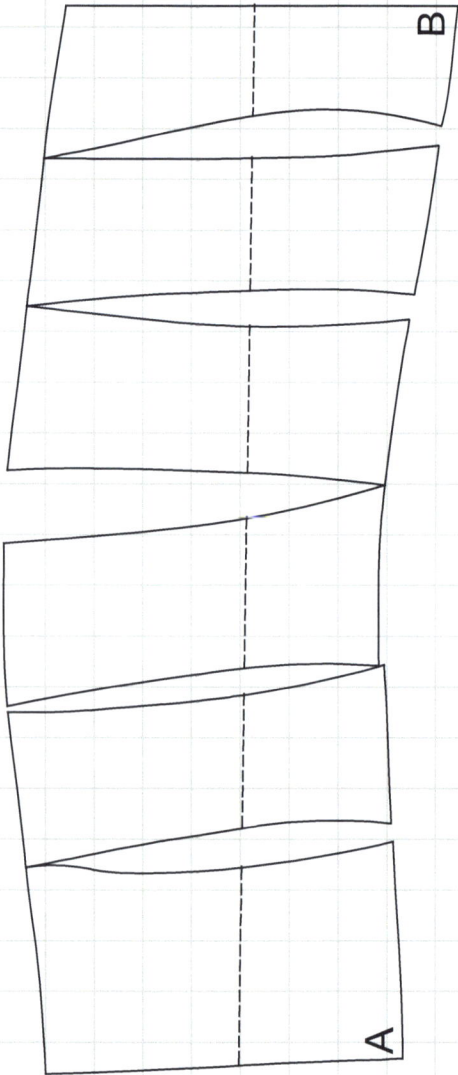

Back

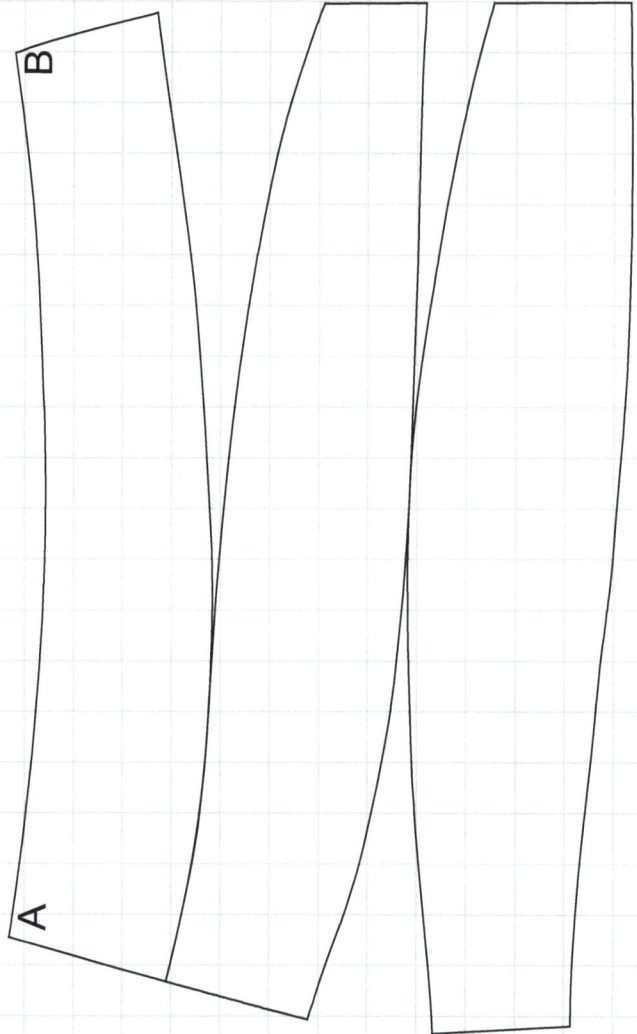

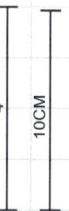

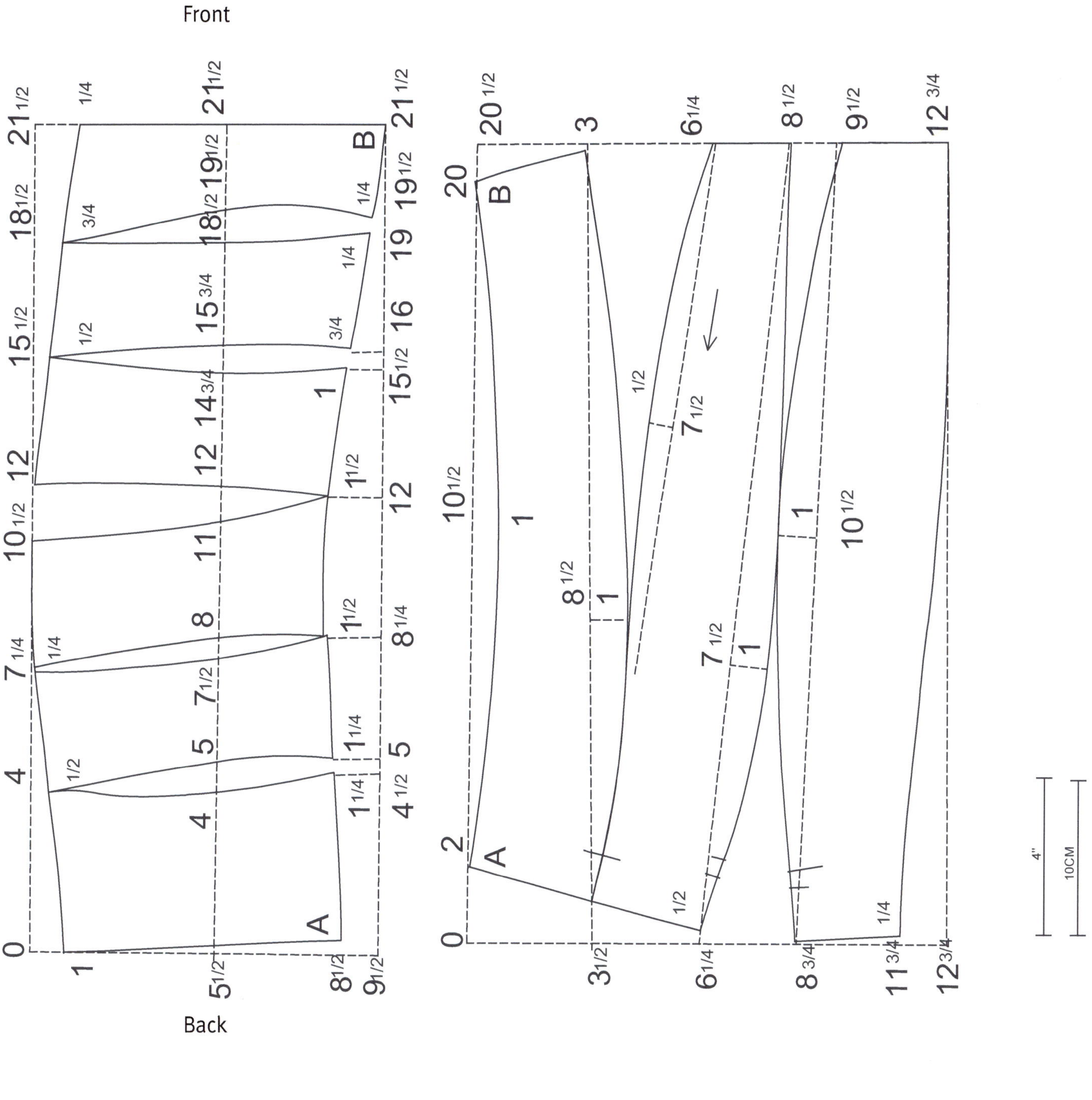

Front

Back

21 1/2   1/4
18 1/2   3/4   21 1/2
21   19 1/2
15 1/2   1/2   15 3/4   18 1/2 19 1/2   B
12   14 3/4   19   21 1/2
10 1/2   11   12   16   19 1/2
7 1/4   1/4   8   15 1/2
4   5   7 1/2   12   1
1/2   1   1 1/2   8 1/4   1/4
0   4   1 1/4   1 1/2   5
1   1 1/4   4 1/2   A
5 1/2   1 1/4
8 1/2
9 1/2

20 1/2
20   B   3
10 1/2   1   6 1/4
8 1/2   1/2   8 1/2
2   A   1   7 1/2   9 1/2
7 1/2   1   12 3/4
3 1/2   1/2   1   10 1/2
6 1/4   1
8 3/4   1
0   11 3/4   1/4
12 3/4

4"
10CM

VIVIAN

A corset which gives full freedom to every movement of the body, yet maintains all the essentials for supporting the body of the person whilst engaged in athletics and various forms of sport, is a desideratum much appreciated by ladies who indulge in these more or less forms of violent exercise. More particularly is the wearing of such a garment important in the case of young persons constitutionally weak, or those whose muscular developments have not yet fully matured.

Stiff, tight-fitting corsets, and those types which are only suitable for walking, or some similar form of gentle exercise, should not be worn when indulging in these more active forms of recreations. It is not only the mischief caused at the time, but memories of the error are often forced into the mind of the unfortunate sufferer later on. It will be seen from the set of patterns that the corset illustrated is very short, both above and below the waist-line. This enables the wearer to bring the body into any position with perfect ease, and give full play to the limbs without encumbrance, however strenuous the exercise may be.

Front of corset 12 1/2 inches; back, 13 inches,. busk, 9 inches ; front linings, are cut 12 3/4 by 1 1/2 inches ; back linings 13 1/4 by 1 3/4 inches; facings for the front are also cut 12 3/4 by 1 1/2 ins; 3 3/4 inch elastic is used.

The patterns are for a corset 23 inches at waist.

The work of making up the corset is similar to what has already appeared on previous pages, with a few exceptions. The facings are joined to the linings in place of the front sections, and the busks put in in the usual way. They are then joined to the fronts by putting the latter between them and stitching. The tops of the facing and lining are neatly folded inside and stitched, and usually left slightly above the elastic gore.

Binding on the corset commences at the other end of gore, and is carried round to the back in the usual way, and the bottoms are bound like the ordinary corsets.

It will be noticed that the narrow stiffeners extend right to the top of the elastic. The strapping is cut long enough to turn the end of it inside and finish neatly, just level with the top of the gore. A neat bow of dainty ribbon is the only trimming this kind of corset requires.

WWI brought many changes to women's wardrobes, and one of them was that sporting clothes became popular to wear everyday, and not just while playing a sport. The clothes were designed to allow a woman to move, and a sport corset was designed to support her figure, hold up the stockings, and also allow for freedom of movement.

"the fact remains that the very reason for the sports costume is freedom, and that is the keynote of the corset which forms the very foundation of the sports ensemble."[47]
Dry Goods Economist, February 18, 1922

This corset dates to 1919 to 1922, and is very similar in dimensions and shape to the 1921 Ferris sport corset, seen below, although with a much deeper elastic section. Sports corsets were not just recommended for sporting activities, but also motoring, and for active occupations, such as nursing, which involved bending and twisting.

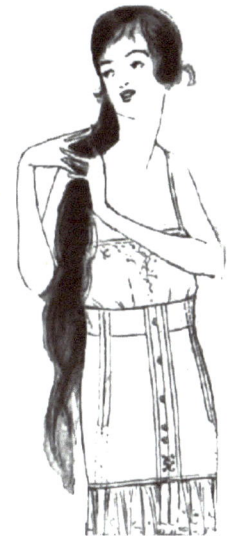

"SPORTS WILL BE MORE THAN EVER POPULAR THIS SEASON. A VERY ATTRACTIVE SPORTS CORSET WHICH COMBINES DAINTINESS, SHAPELINESS, AND DURABILITY IS SHOWN AT THE LEFT. IT IS MADE OF PALE PINK SATIN, THE HEAVY, WASHABLE SATIN WITH MERCERIZED BACK WHICH IS WOVEN ESPECIALLY FOR CORSETS. IT IS VERY LIGHTLY BONED, AND THE SHORTNESS AND THE DEEP BAND OF ELASTIC AT THE TOP COMBINE TO GIVE GREAT FREEDOM TO THE WEARER WHEN SHE IS ACTIVE IN ANY SPORT." GOOD HOUSEKEEPING, APRIL 1919 P.64

STYLE 372 - PINK TRECO STYLE 370 - WHITE COUTIL SIZES 20 TO 30 INCHES. ABOVE THE WAIST LINE THERE IS A TWO INCH STRIP OF MERCERIZED ELASTIC WEBBING. VERY LOW BUST, MEDIUM LENGTH HIP. LIGHT BONING. FRONT LENGTH 11 INCHES. BACK LENGTH 12 1/2 INCHES. 8 1/2 IN. FLEXIBLE CLASP FRONT. ONE HOOK BELOW THE CLASP. LACING AT THE BACK. FERRIS CORSET CATALOG 1921

ATHLETIC MODEL 23R3046 PINK BROCADE PRICE $1.19 FOR THE ENERGETIC OR ATHLETIC WOMAN HERE IS A COMFORTABLE MODEL IN A SERVICEABLE AND ATTRACTIVE BROCADE. THE FLESH COLORED RUBBER TOP GIVES FREELY AND DOES NOT BIND; RUSTPROOF BONING THROUGHOUT; LONG OVER THE HIPS. FOUR GOOD HOSE SUPPORTERS. NO BONING OVER THE LONG HIPS. SIZES 20-30 CHARLES WILLIAMS CATALOG, 1922

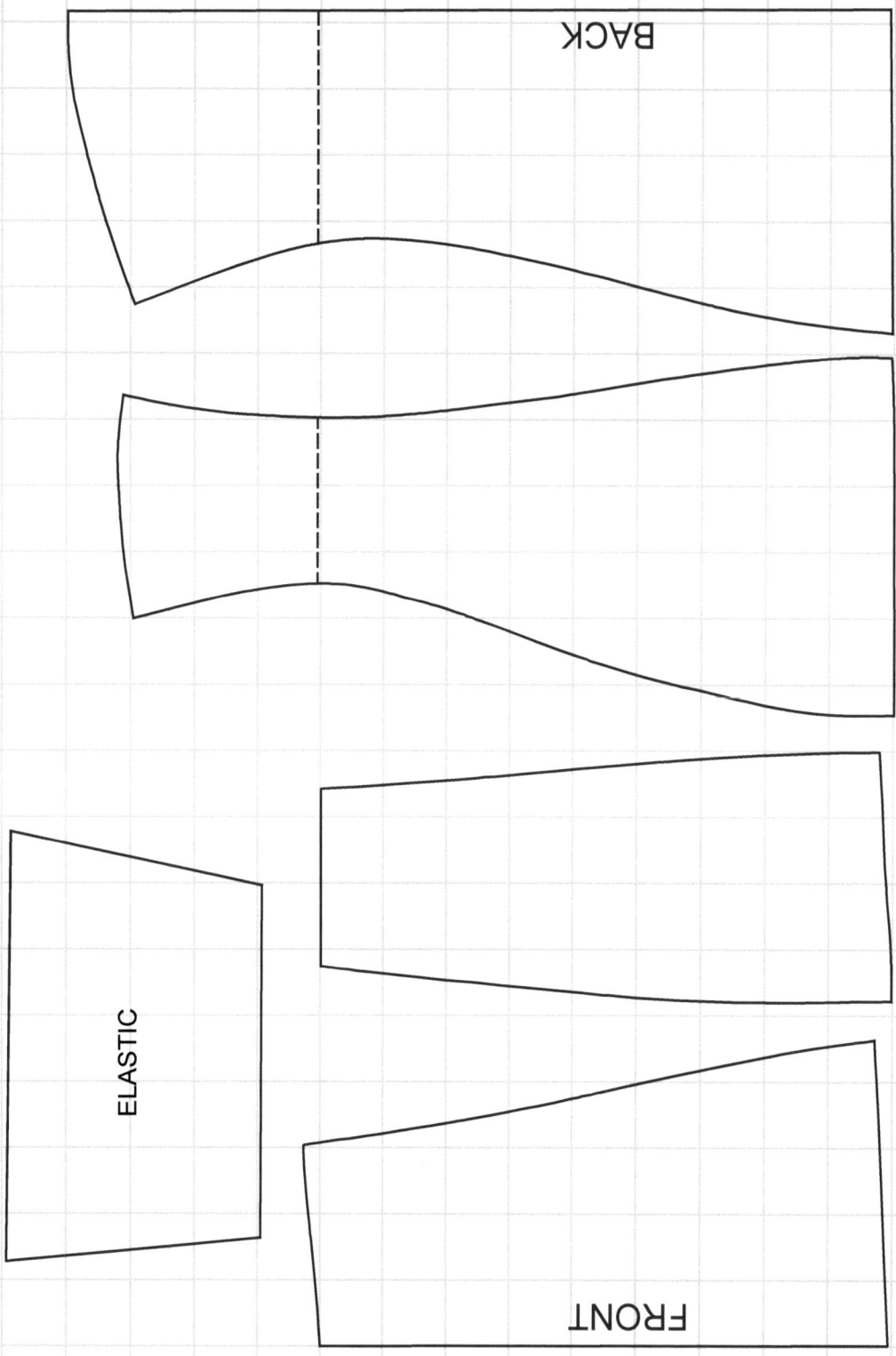

BACK

ELASTIC

FRONT

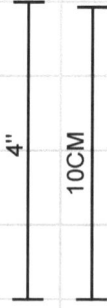

4"

10CM

NOT SHOWN ON DIAGRAM: BUSK FACING AND LINING, BOTH 12 3/4 BY 1 1/2 INCHES;
BACK LININGS FOR LACING STRIP 13 1/4 BY 1 3/4 INCHES.

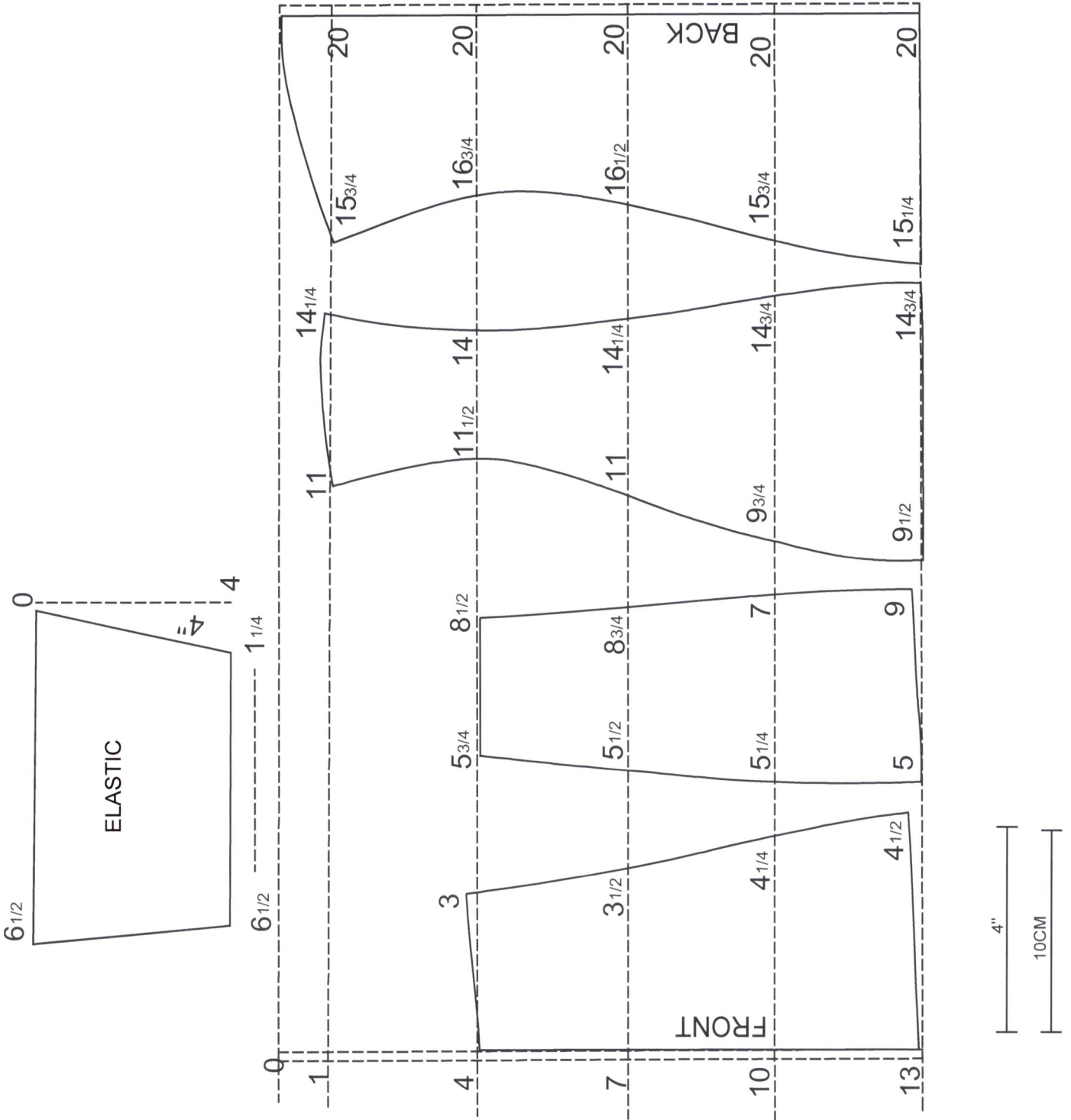

BACK

FRONT

ELASTIC

6 1/2

0

4

4"

1 1/4

6 1/2

20 20 20 20 20

15 3/4 16 3/4 16 1/2 15 3/4 15 1/4

14 1/4 14 14 1/4 14 3/4 14 3/4

11 11 1/2 11 9 3/4 9 1/2

8 1/2 8 3/4 7 9

5 3/4 5 1/2 5 1/4 5

3 3 1/2 4 1/4 4 1/2

4"

10CM

0

1

4

7

10

13

CORSET WAISTS FOR CHILDREN AND MAIDS

1886-1921

Ferris'
GOOD SENSE
Corset Waists.

SENSIBLE WOMEN WEAR THEM

BECAUSE THEY ARE {RIGHT RIGHT RIGHT}
Shape to fit properly and feel comfortable
Material to give the best service.
Finish because of skilled labor.
Buttons and Button Holes won't pull off.
Support from the shoulders.
Fastenings for Hose Supporters.

Why Buy an Imitation when the GENUINE Costs so Little and Wears so Long?
CHILDREN'S, 25c. to 75c. MISSES, 50c. to $1. LADIES, $1 to $2.

FERRIS CORSET WAIST ADVERTISEMENT
LADIES WORLD, 1895

Long before Symington's started selling their famous "Liberty Bodice" in the early 1900s, several US and Canadian companies were selling "waists" or "corset waists". Ferris Good Sense Waist Co is probably the best known company among the many companies who sold different types of corded waists for children of all ages, and grown women, beginning in the late 1870s to mid-1880s.

Waists were advertised as being essential to good health, and as an aid in shaping a child's figure, while allowing for total freedom and comfort.

"Careful attention to the young girl's corseting to-day means an attractive figure for her at maturity. The Ferris Waist for growing girls allows perfect freedom and comfort and at the same time develops the form into graceful lines.
For the younger ones the soft waists with no boning are used"
Ferris Good Sense Catalog, 1921

The key to achieving this freedom of movement was a good fit. The lead buyer of corsets and corset waists at Best & Co. had this to say about the proper fit of children's waists:

"To a casual observer, it would seem of little importance that the waist should fit too snugly over the diaphragm, the straps be a bit too long or short, the top too high or the skirt not exactly the right length. We fully realize, however, what these details mean to the child or young girl, for points of seemingly little importance have much to do with the shaping of little figures, their manner of walking, or even the position they take while sitting.
One of the most essential requirements is plenty of breadth over the diaphragm. An uncomfortable pressure at this point causes the most disastrous results. In older persons this fault is quickly remedied by the selection of a different style of corset, but the ordinary child does not realize what the difficulty really is, and tries to hold the little body in a position which best relieves the pressure. This usually means a

slight throwing forward of the shoulders and holding in of the body at the waist, a position, if followed for any time, produces an ungraceful stoop of the body and an undesirable way of walking, to say nothing of the real injury to the child in not having the lungs, heart and diaphragm absolutely free.

It is important to have a waist fit easily over the abdomen, particularly for young girls; and also that no boning comes over the hip, as this part of the body should be absolutely free to respond to every body movement."

Dry Goods Economist, v.66 Feb. 17, 1912 p.47

On the next page:

Child's Corset Waist, for up to 7 years old

This child's waist is very similar to many found in catalogs from the 1900 through the early 1920s, and could button in the front or the back. It could be worn by either boys or girls, and was available in a range of fabrics. It had buttons on the bottom edge to attach underwear and outer clothes, as elastic waistbands were not in use at this time. The buttons were attached with a cloth tape, not sewn on with thread, for extra reliability, and the buttonholes were made from strips of fabric, as shown right, from the original 1886 Ferris Bros. patent, US 345037.

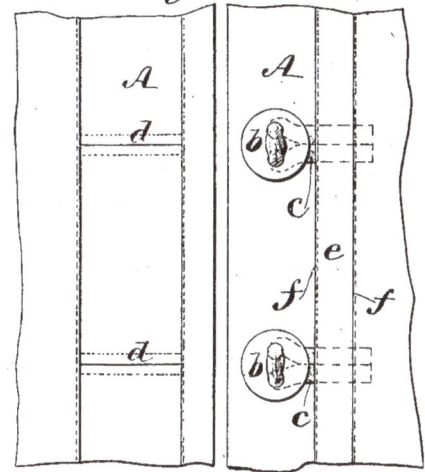

HOW THE BUTTONS ARE ATTACHED, USING FERRIS BROS' PATENTED TAPE METHOD, PATENT US 345037

BOYS' WAISTS
STYLE 159 SIZES 2 TO 10 YEARS
STRONG TWILL. BUTTONS AT FRONT, CLOSED BACK. BUTTONS FOR DRAWERS AND PANTS. NO HOSE SUPPORTERS. FERRIS PATENT, TAPE-FASTENED, BONE BUTTONS. FERRIS CORSET WAIST CATALOG, 1921

FOR CHILDREN 4 TO 14 YEARS
STYLE 504 SIZES 4 TO 10. 12 AND 14 YEARS
FINE BATISTE. NEATLY CORDED. TRIMMED WITH EDGING. BUTTONS UP THE BACK, CLOSED FRONT. BUTTONS FOR SKIRTS AND DRAWERS. FERRIS PATENT TAPE-FASTENED BONE BUTTONS. FERRIS CORSET WAIST CATALOG, 1921

CHILD'S CORSET WAIST

FOR UP TO 7 YEARS OLD

The pattern of for a child's corset is suitable for a child up to seven years of age. It may be made to lace down the back, which is an advantage, as it allows for expansion as the child grows.

Before cutting out the corsets it is advisable to cut all strips for strapping and buttonhole pieces.

About four yards of strapping cut 1 inch will be wanted. Fold each edge over 1/4 inch, which will bring them to the centre and make nice firm supports 1/2 inch wide. The stability of the corset is thus provided for, and there is no risk of frayed edges appearing.

When the corset is made in "Molleton" a firm white binding 1/2 inch wide is used in place of the strapping. Buttonhole strips are cut two inches wide, all edges turned and made up double, then cut into pieces 1 1/4 inches long. The button piece must also be made from double material 1 1/4 inches wide when folded. Seam the various sections together and then strap them. All strapping is stitched on to the outside of corset.

Commence by sewing the two belt strips on first, then strap the seams. The button and buttonhole pieces are next joined to their respective parts. Cut a piece of the material for binding the buttonhole pieces, 1 1/8 inches wide, and fold the edges nearly to the centre. This makes a very firm binding to resist the strain. Strap the seams in the usual way. The buttons are put on with narrow tape. Thread the tape through the buttonholes and leave the ends long enough to be sewn under the strapping when the seam is being covered. The shoulder straps are next seamed.

Binding the corset is the next operation, then put two buttons on each side where the second seams are crossed by the belt seams, and the corset will be completed.

Shoulder straps may be made with button holes, as shown, or left with plain points and the adjustment made with a safety-pin.

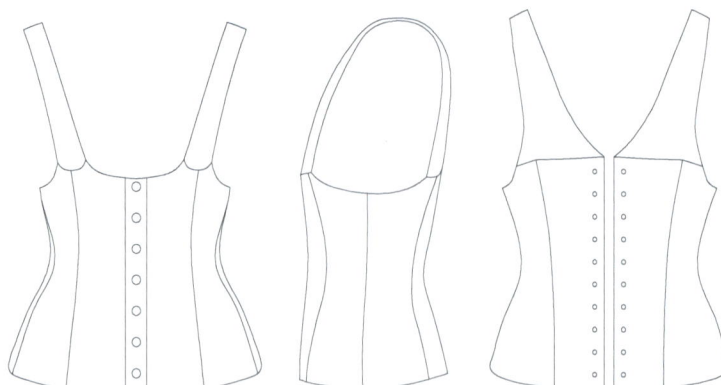

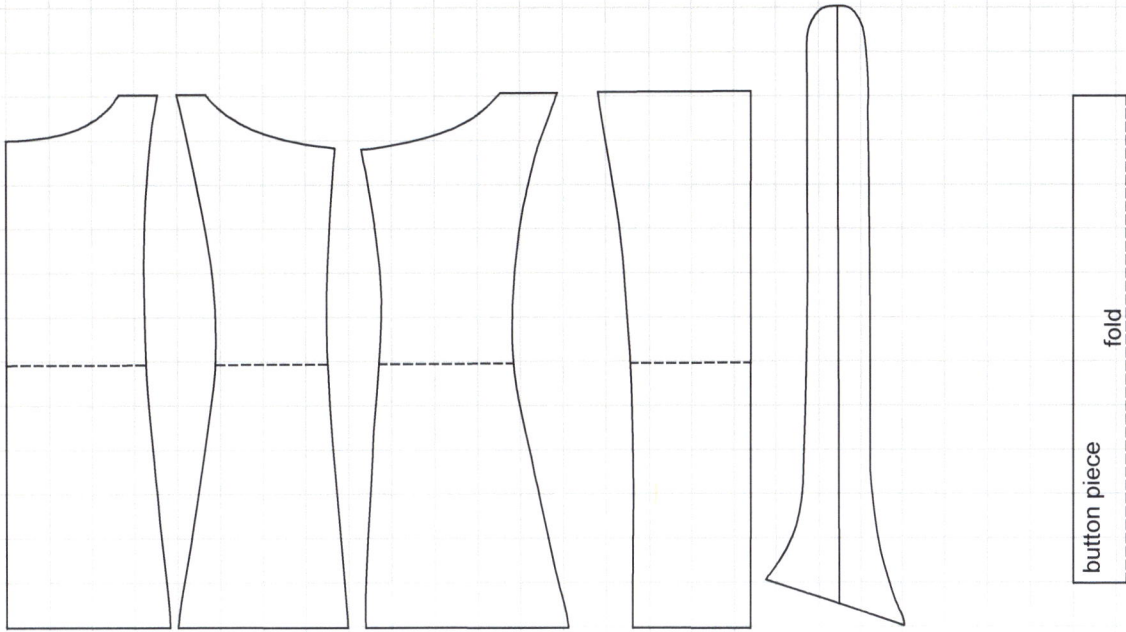

button piece

fold

4"

10CM

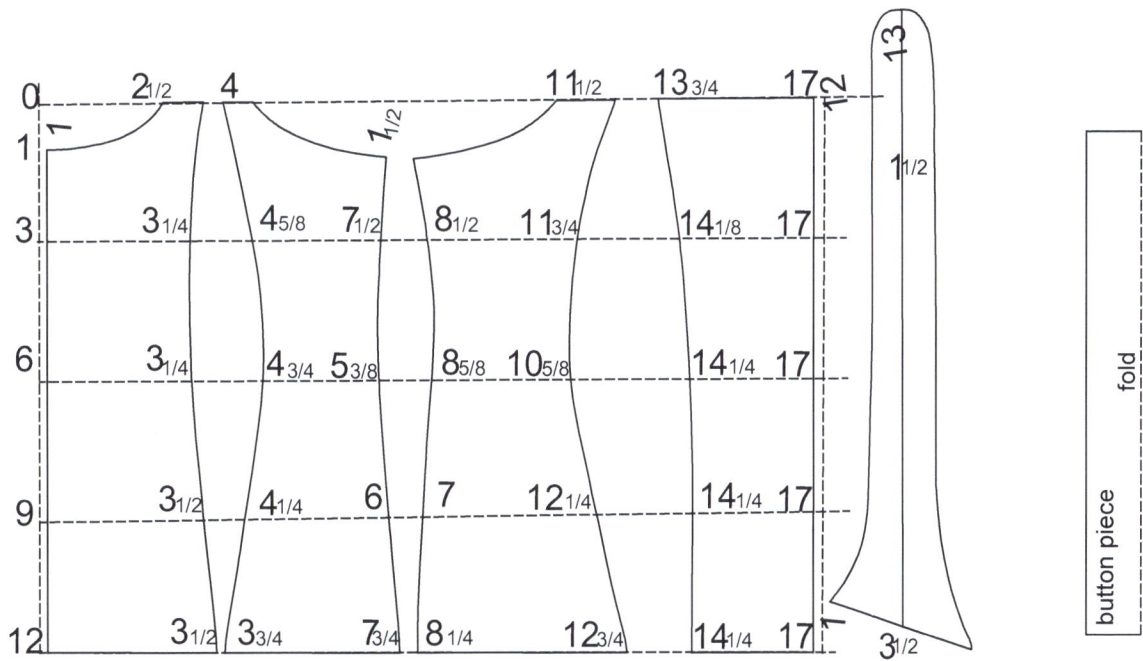

button piece

fold

4"

10CM

GIRL'S CORSET WAIST
FOR 7 TO 17 YEARS OLD

Maids and growing children require corsets that in no way restrict their actions or impede their growth and development. These shown on the accompanying diagram and illustration afford perfect freedom of movement, and also provide the necessary support. The diagram explains how to reproduce them, and the various points may be readily followed.

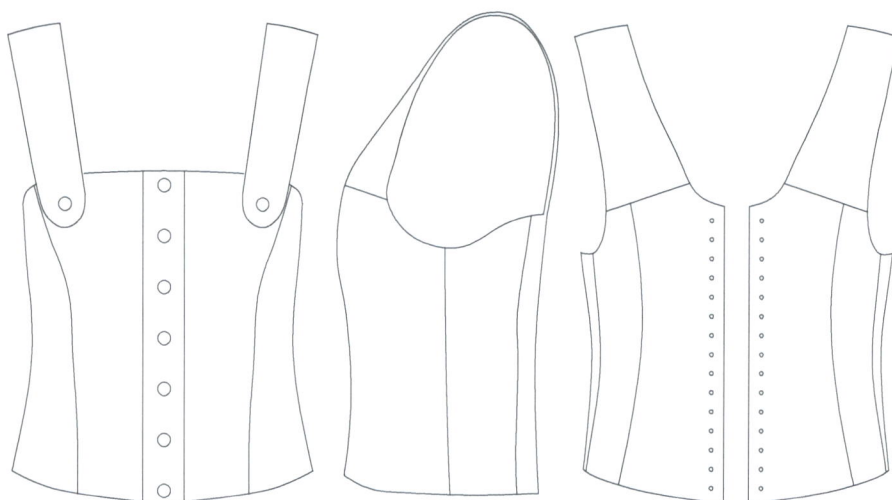

This was the most common style of children's waist available in catalogs from 1895-1920, and was worn by girls and misses up to 17 years old, with a more shapely version available for women.

This waist used the same button and button placket design seen in the other children's waists, and would have been corded, not boned. It was mainly a garment to provide an extra layer of warmth, and a way to hold stockings up before the era of elastic waistbands.

FOR MISSES 7-11 YEARS
STYLE 704 - TWILL BUTTONS UP THE FRONT
STYLE 804 - TWILL CLASP FRONT (9 1/2 IN.)
DESIGNED TO FIT THE CHILD'S FIGURE. NEATLY CORDED. BONED UNDER THE FRONT BUTTONS AND AT THE BACK LACING. SHOULDER STRAPS PROPERLY CURVED TO FIT. FERRIS PATENT, TAPE-FASTENED, BONE BUTTONS. LACING AT THE BACK. BUTTONS ON EACH HIP FOR FASTENING CLOTHING. ONE PAIR DOUBLE HOSE SUPPORTERS.

(SIMILAR STYLES AVAILABLE IN TWILL AND BATISTE FOR MISSES 10 TO 14 AND 14 TO 17 YEARS OLD)
FERRIS CORSET WAIST CATALOG, 1921

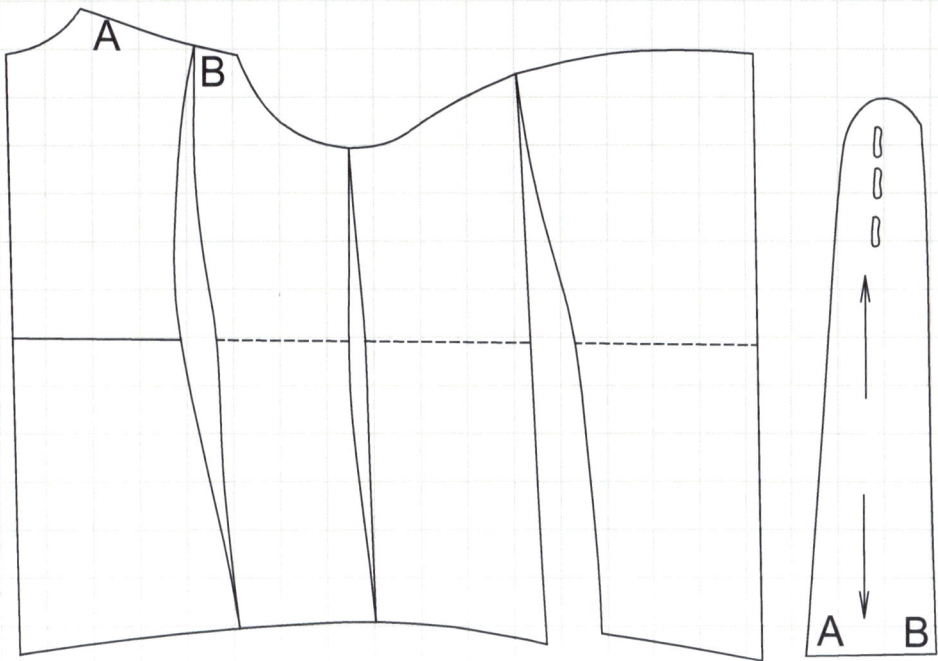

4"

10CM

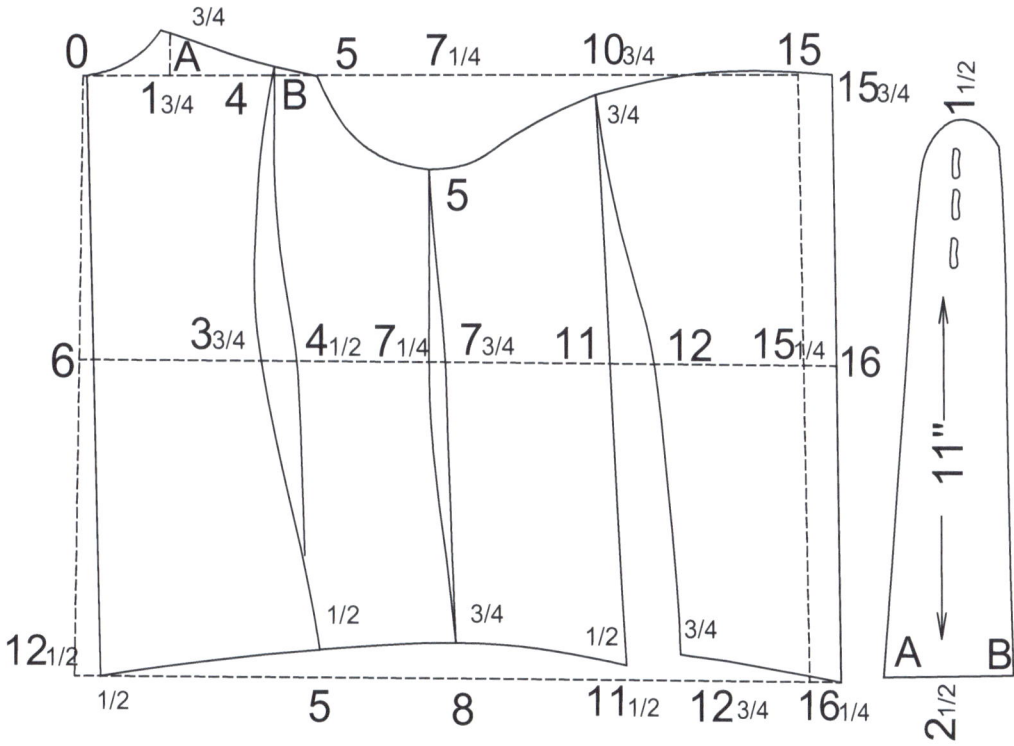

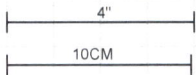

0   3/4
A   5   7 1/4   10 3/4   15
1 3/4   4   B   15 3/4
3/4
5

6   3 3/4   4 1/2   7 1/4   7 3/4   11   12   15 1/4   16

1 1/2

11"

A   B

12 1/2   1/2   3/4   1/2   3/4   2 1/2
1/2   5   8   11 1/2   12 3/4   16 1/4

4"

10CM

GIRL'S CORSET WAIST

11 TO 15 YEARS OLD 1886-1907

The maid's corset shown is suitable for girls 11 to 15 years of age, and the construction of it is in many respects similar to the foregoing.

Shoulder straps are dispensed with, which gives the corset a more fashionable appearance without disturbing its qualities as a healthful and comfortable garment. In making up the corset it is advisable to carry out all possible work on the front and back pieces before seaming the parts together, Button and buttonhole pieces can be finished throughout and strapped, and the backs lined and eyelets put in. The front and second pieces are next seamed together, and the third and back pieces. The two parts are next joined at the shoulder and the seam covered. Strapping is then stitched over the long seams, starting at the bottom of one part, carried over the shoulder, and finishing at the other end of seam. The arm holes are next bound, starting at the unseamed point under arm and carried round to the opposite point. The side seams are then stitched and strapped, and the curved strapping sewn on. Bind the top and bottom and sew on the buttons for knickers.

Trim with lace or embroidery, and complete it by putting on suspenders.

THE S&S VESTINA CORSET BODICE
A SOFT FINISHED WASHING BODICE.
STRAIGHT 10" BUSK, CHILDS 2/3
STRAIGHT 11" BUSK, GIRLS 2/6
STRAIGHT 12 1/2" BUSK, MAIDS 2/9
STRAIGHT 12 BUSK, YOUNG LADIES 3/9
ARMY NAVY STORES CATALOG (UK),
1907

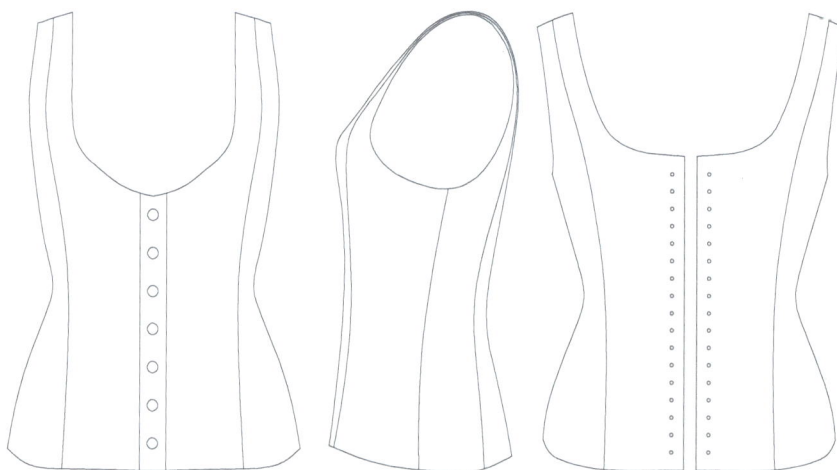

This style of corset bodice is first seen in an 1885 Ferris Good Sense Corset Waist advertisement, and was available from them through 1890. A very similar bodice was also advertised by the S&S company as the "Vestina Corset Bodice", in New Zealand in 1900[50] and the United Kingdom in 1907[51].

It was designed to be a supportive garment to help a young woman with her figure, and also support a growing bust. It could either button or have a busk.

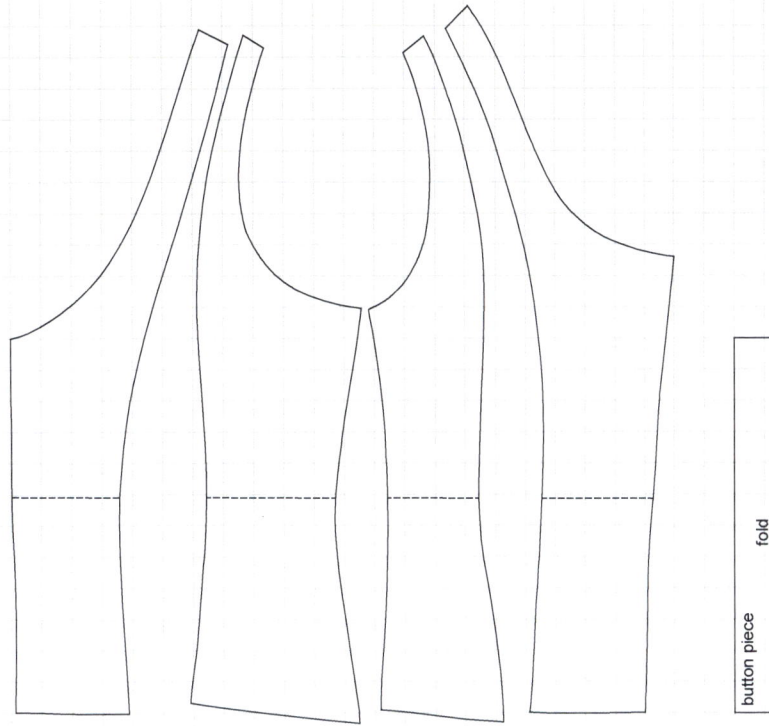

fold

button piece

4"
10CM

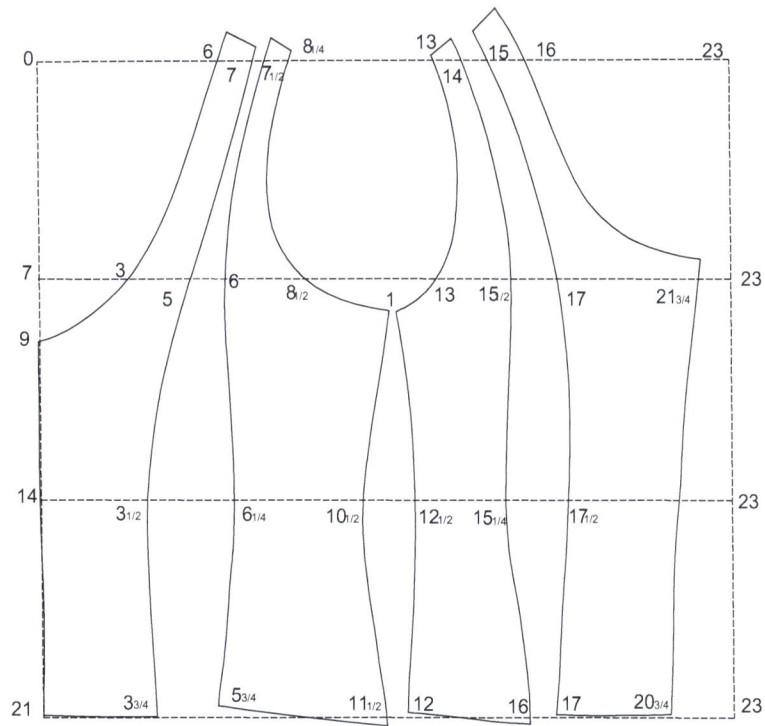

| | | | | | | | |
0   6   7   7½   8¼   13   14   15   16   23

7   3   5   6   8½   1   13   15½   17   21¾   23

9

14   3½   6¼   10½   12½   15¼   17½   23

21   3¾   5¾   11½   12   16   17   20¾   23

4"
10CM

111

Appendix

Measuring

The measurements needed for a proper fitting corset change depending on the style of corset, and so with the change in styles the necessary measurements change. As the length of the corset changed above and below the waist, a different set of measurements was needed to achieve a perfect fit, especially after 1910 as the corset lengthened over the hips. Here are two sets of instructions for taking measurements from 1902[48], and 1924[49] which cover the styles of corset found in this book.

1902 Bon Marche Measures for Custom Corsets

1) Waist

2) Chest and back, passing under the arms

3) Hips, at the widest place

4) Length of the busk from the top of the corset to the waist

4) Length of the busk from the waist to the bottom edge

5) Height under the arm, from the top of the corset to the waist

6) Width of half of chest from the middle of the chest to the edge of the arm.

7) Height of the back, from the scapula to the waist

The hip measurement must always be taken at the widest place, whether it be a short or long corset; It is sufficient that our Client tells us if she wants her corset to be short or long on the hips.

SPIRELLA MEASUREMENTS, 1916-1924

These measurement instructions are from Spirella Instruction Book, Fifth Edition, dated 1924. They are nearly identical to the ones found in their 1916 instruction manual.

Section 8 – How to Take Measurements

1. Certain anatomical points determine the location of the measurements and they must be taken at the same places, and in the same way on each client. This is necessary in order that the Corsetiere and the Company may get the same visualization, and in order that they may work from the same standpoint.

Note: The measurements are always taken to certain definite points on the body as illustrated in the following pages, regardless of the height or length of the corset over which the measurements are taken, or the height or length to be ordered. The measurements taken are actual body measurements and should not be confused with corset measurements.

2. Measuring the client is divided into four general steps as follows:
   · Measurements around the body
   · Measurements above the waist line
   · Measurements below the waist line
   · Measurements with the client in the sitting position

Measurements Around the Body

(Taken with Client in Correct Standing Position)

3. Waist (indicated by the line W-W on Diagram R).

The waist line is the base from which all up and down measurements are taken; therefore the waist measurement must be taken first. Place buckle-end tape line around the waist, following the natural poise or slant of the client's waist line. Then draw it snugly and fasten. Tuck the loose end in the top of the corset. This tape line must remain fixed until all measurements are taken.

4. Bust (indicated by line B-B on Diagram R). Stand at one side slightly behind your client, place the tape line over the fullest part of the bust and around the body at about the same distance from the waist line all around, and take the measurement smoothly, never tightly.

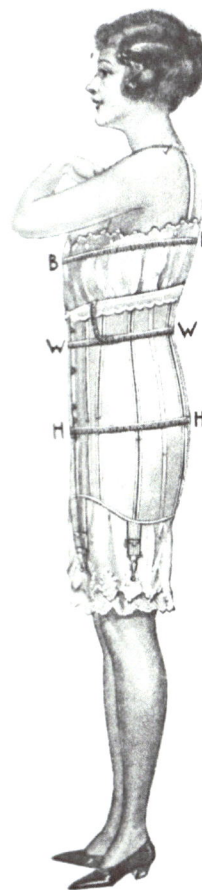

DIAGRAM R

(Note: Present day corsets do not extend to the client's bust line, but regardless of the height to which the corset is to be made, the bust measurement must always be taken at the fullest part of the bust.)

5. Hip (indicated by line H-H on Diagram R). To insure accuracy place pins 6 1/2 inches below the waist line in front, at the sides and in the back; measure around the hips over these pins, drawing the tape line tightly. Remove the pins after taking the measurement.

Measurements above the waist

(Taken with Client in Correct Standing Position)

6. Center Front Above Waist (indicated by line 1-2 on Diagram S). Measure from the bottom of the tape line at the waist up to the level of the measurement taken around fullest part of the bust. (See B-B Diagram R.)

7. Center Bust (indicated by line 3-4 on Diagram S). Measure from bottom of the tape line at the waist up to the center of the breast - the level of the measurement taken around the fullest part of the bust.

8. Under Arm (indicated by line 5-6 on Diagram S). Measure from bottom of the tape line at the waist up to the level of the measurement taken around the fullest part of the bust. The client's arm should not be raised while taking this measurement.

9. Back Above Waist (indicated by line 7-8 on Diagram T). Measure from bottom of the tape line at the waist straight up to the level of the measurement taken around the fullest part of the bust. This measurement is taken about two inches to one side of the center back.

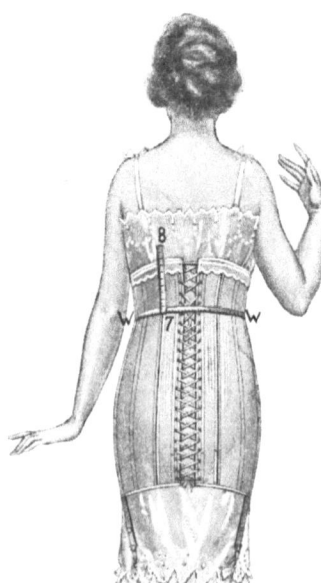

DIAGRAM S   DIAGRAM T   DIAGRAM U

Measurements Below Waist

(Taken with Client in Correct Standing Position)

10. Back Below Waist (indicated by line 9-10 on Diagram U). Measure from bottom of the tape line at the waist straight down over the back hip to the back of the leg, entirely covering the curve of the flesh. The measurement is taken directly under the measurement for back above waist line.

11. Hip Length (indicated by line 11-12 on Diagram V). Measure from bottom of the tape line at the waist straight down over the side hip to a point on the leg, sufficiently low to cover the curve of the flesh.

12. Groin Lengths (indicated by line 13-14-15 on Diagram V). Measure from bottom of the tape line at the waist down to the groin (bend of the leg just above the thigh) and from there down to a point on the leg sufficiently low to cover any flesh necessary to control. This gives two lengths; the true groin lenght (see Diagram V) and the length to cover leg flesh.

13. Center Front Below Waist (indicated by line 16-17 on Diagram V). Measure from bottom of the tape line at the waist down to the upper edge of the pelvic arch. Draw the tape line taut to get a flat measurement. The center front below waist helps you decide the length of the clasp below waist. For further instructions on how to take this measurement, and locate the upper edge of the pelvic arch, see paragraph 15.

14. The illustrations of the skeletal fram (Diagrams 5 and 6) show a front and side view of the pelvic girdle. This is known as the pelvis. It is a basin-shaped, bony cavity formed by three bones - the lower part of the spine in the center back and the hip bones on each side joining the spine. The hip bones curve toward the front and there unity to form what is called the pelvic arch.

15. To locate the pelvic arch, place your right hand on your client's back hip, take the tape line between the thumb and first finger of the left hand, about five inches from the end that you are measuring with. Place this hand up under the skirt of the corset. Press gently inward and downward on the flesh of the lower part of the abdomen until you touch the upper edge of the bones forming the arch. Bring your thumb down to this point, and with the right hand draw the tape line up through your fingers until you reach the bottom edge of the waist tape. Draw the tape measure taut and it will give you an accurate center front below waist measurement.

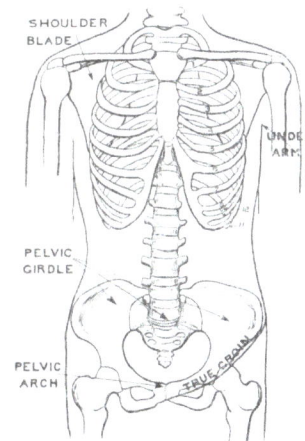

DIAGRAM 5

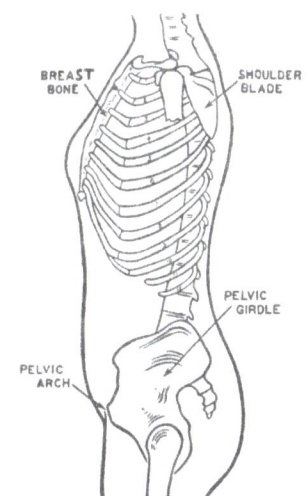

DIAGRAM 6

Tested Center Bust and Boning Lenths

16. Tested Center Bust (indicated by line from 18 (at waist) to center bust on Diagram W F). Test the center bust measurement in the sitting position as the client's flesh often settles when she is seated, and thus gives a shorter measurement than the one taken in standing position.

17. Groin Boning (indicated by line 18-19 on Diagram W F). Measure from bottom of the tape line at the waist to a point just above the true groin line. Draw the tape line taut to get a flat measurement. The groin boning length is usually about one inch shorter than the center front measurement below waist, expect in cases of prominent or pendulous abdomen.

18. Back Boning (indicated by line 20-21 on Diagram W B). Measure from bottom of the tape line at the waist over the curve of the hips in the back. Boning should be short enough to escape the chair.

19. As the different measurements are taken, write them down in your order book, in the spaces provided for the client's actual body measurements. Your order book then gives you an accurate record of her body measurements and figure description. This is essential to assist you in selecting the corset which will best care for your client's needs.

20. By "body measurements", "actual body measurements" or "actual measurements" we mean the client's measurements taken as outlined in Section Eight over a well-prepared foundation, which is obtained by correctly adjusting a corset as outlined in Section Seven. We do not mean measurements taken over the body uncorseted.

DIAGRAM V

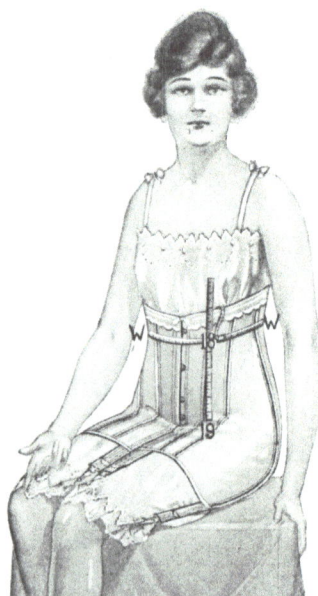

DIAGRAM W F

DIAGRAM W B

Serafina
Savoy Satin in Mauritius, by James Hare
Lace from LaceTime on Etsy
Corset constructed by Nikki Swift, Narrowed Visions Corsets
photography by Nikki Swift

NOTES

1 Corset Fashions for 1914, Les Dessous Elegants, January 1914
   HTTPS://COMMONS.WIKIMEDIA.ORG/WIKI/FILE:LESDESSOUSELEGANTSJANVIER1914PAGE3.PNG

2 Corset and Underwear Review, July 1921, p.38
   HTTPS://BOOKS.GOOGLE.COM/BOOKS?ID=A4M1AQAAMAAJ&PG=RA3-PA38

3 The Vincent Conglomeration, W.D.F. Vincent, Tailor and Journalist
   HTTPS://WWW.VINCENTS.ORG.UK/FAMILY-HISTORY/W-D-F-VINCENT-TAILOR

4 The Corset and Underwear Review, January 1916, p.39
   HTTPS://HDL.HANDLE.NET/2027/NYP.33433057680757?URLAPPEND=%3BSEQ=378

5 Canadian Dry Goods Review, August 1917 p.91
   HTTPS://ARCHIVE.ORG/STREAM/DGRSTYLE1917TORO#PAGE/N1103/MODE/2UP/

6 The Corset and Underwear Review. v. 10, October 1917 p.42
   HTTPS://HDL.HANDLE.NET/2027/NYP.33433090823828?URLAPPEND=%3BSEQ=50

7 Dry Goods Economist, v.63, issue2, July 31, 1909 p.47
   HTTPS://HDL.HANDLE.NET/2027/UIUG.30112064273631?URLAPPEND=%3BSEQ=583

8 Dry Goods Economist, v.63, issue2, August 7, 1909 p.47
   HTTPS://BABEL.HATHITRUST.ORG/CGI/PT?ID=UIUG.30112064273631;VIEW=1UP;SEQ=671

9 Spirella 1913 Manual:
   HTTPS://EN.WIKISOURCE.ORG/WIKI/SPIRELLA_MANUAL_(1913)/SECTION_3

10 1902 Sears Catalog,p.1102 Her Ladyship corset listing
   HTTPS://ARCHIVE.ORG/DETAILS/CATALOGUENO11200SEAR

11 Macy's 1911 Catalog, p.139 listing for Marchioness corset
   HTTPS://ARCHIVE.ORG/DETAILS/CATALOGUENO16SPR00MACY

12 Spirella 1913 Manual
   Ferris Patent, US 1193790 HTTPS://WWW.GOOGLE.COM/PATENTS/US1193790
   Ferris Patent, US 1193742 HTTPS://WWW.GOOGLE.COM/PATENTS/US1193742
   National Cloak & Suit Catalog, 1918 p.264

13 Minimum Wage Commission, Bulletin No.2, January 1914: Wages of Women in the Corset Factories in Massachusetts
   HTTPS://BOOKS.GOOGLE.COM/BOOKS?ID=WI5QAAAAYAAJ&PG=PP33

14 1913 Report on Conditions of Woman and Child Wage Earners in the United States in Selected Industries, Volume 18
   HTTPS://BOOKS.GOOGLE.COM/BOOKS?ID=QX03AQAAIAAJ&PG=PA148

15 1914 report

16 Ibid.

17 1913 report

18 1914 report

19 Ibid.

20 Ibid.

21 Ibid.

22 1913 report

23 1914 report

24 Ibid.

25 Ibid

26 Ibid

27 1913 report

28 1914 report

29 Ibid

30 1904 General Price List of Jeremiah Rotherman & Co
   HTTP://WWW.ARCHIVE.ORG/STREAM/GENERALPRICELIST00JERE#PAGE/452/MODE/2UP

31 "In the Matter of Bayer's Design" Reports of Patent, Design, Trade Mark, and Other Cases, Volumes 23-24, Oct. 17, 1906, p.566
   HTTPS://BOOKS.GOOGLE.COM/BOOKS?ID=PO5CAQAAMAAJ&PG=PA566

32 Weinberg's cloak, skirt and cape cutter, 1900 p.8
   HTTPS://ARCHIVE.ORG/DETAILS/WEINBERGSCLOAKSK00WEIN

33 Dry Goods Reporter, October 1900, p.15
https://books.google.com/books?id=jKE7AQAAMAAJ& pg=RA18-PA15

34 The Overland Monthly, August 1900, p.172
https://books.google.com/books?id=7dVD5ri-T3wC&pg=PA172

35 The American Horsewoman, Elizabeth Karr 1890 p.60-61
https://archive.org/stream/americanhorsewom00karrrich#page/60

36 The Horsewoman: A Practical Guide to Side-saddle Riding By Alice M. Hayes 1903
https://books.google.com/books?id=NtY8AAAAYAAJ

37 Les Dessous Elegants, 1906 No.7 p.109
https://upload.wikimedia.org/wikipedia/commons/3/34/LesDessousElegants1906page109.png

38 Salen, Jill. Corsets: Historic Patterns and Techniques. London: Batsford, 2008. p59

39 The Dry Goods Reporter, Vol 46 issue 1, Jan 16 1915
https://books.google.com/books?id=4cgcAQAAMAAJ&pg=PA122

40 Dry Goods Economist, Dec. 1911, p.155
https://hdl.handle.net/2027/uiug.30112064273540?urlappend=%3Bseq=513

41 Dry Goods Economist, v.63 August 28, 1909 p.11
https://hdl.handle.net/2027/uiug.30112064273631?urlappend=%3Bseq=993

42 Literary digest, June 1918 letter from woman doctor on the importance of wearing corsets,
and munitions plants, etc.
https://books.google.com/books?id=L4U4AQAAMAAJ&pg=RA1-PA22

43 Delineator, September 1917
https://books.google.com/books?id=BZpJAQAAMAAJ&pg=RA2-PA43

44 Canadian Dry Goods Review, January 1917 p.123
https://archive.org/stream/dgrstyle1917toro#page/n121/mode/2up

45 Delineator, September 1917
https://books.google.com/books?id=BZpJAQAAMAAJ&pg=RA2-PA43

46 The Corset and Underwear Review. v. 11 (1918). April issue, p.90
https://hdl.handle.net/2027/nyp.33433090823869?urlappend=%3Bseq=78

47 Dry Goods Economist, February 18, 1922
https://books.google.com/books?id=HsNFAQAAMAAJ&pg=RA3-PA111

48 1902 Au Bon Marche Measures
https://commons.wikimedia.org/wiki/Category:Au_Bon_March%C3%A9_%E2%80%94_Catalogue_des_Corsets

49 Spirella Instruction Book, Fifth Edition, dated 1924.

50 National Library of New Zealand
http://natlib.govt.nz/records/22530818

51 https://commons.wikimedia.org/wiki/File:TheArmyNavyStoresCatalogue_page779.jpg

REFERENCES

Catalogs

1895-96 Fall and winter price list, Jordan Marsh Catalog, Boston USA
HTTPS://ARCHIVE.ORG/STREAM/FALLWINTER18956P00JORD

1902-1903 Supplementary catalogue: Fall and Winter, 1902-3 Chas. A. Stevens & Bros. (Chicago, Ill.)
HTTPS://ARCHIVE.ORG/DETAILS/SUPPLEMENTARYCAT00CHAS

1902 Catalogue no. 112. by Sears, Roebuck and Company
HTTPS://ARCHIVE.ORG/DETAILS/CATALOGUENO11200SEAR

1904 General Price List, Jeremiah Rotherman & Co.
HTTP://WWW.ARCHIVE.ORG/STREAM/GENERALPRICELIST00JERE

1904 Eaton's Spring and Summer Catalogue 1904
HTTPS://ARCHIVE.ORG/DETAILS/EATONS190400EATOUOFT

1905-1906 Fall- Winter Catalog R. H. Macy & Co.
HTTPS://ARCHIVE.ORG/DETAILS/CATALOGUEFALLWIN00MACY

1907 Catalogue de corsets de Rainal Frères
HTTPS://FR.WIKISOURCE.ORG/WIKI/CATALOGUE_DE_CORSETS_DE_RAINAL_FR%C3%A8RES

1911 Spring- Summer Catalog, R. H. Macy & Co.
HTTPS://ARCHIVE.ORG/DETAILS/CATALOGUENO16SPR00MACY

1912 Catalog no. 124. by Sears, Roebuck and Company
HTTPS://ARCHIVE.ORG/DETAILS/CATALOGNO12400SEAR

Spirella's 1913 Accessories Catalog
HTTPS://EN.WIKISOURCE.ORG/WIKI/INDEX:SPIRELLA_ACCESSORIES_1913

1916 Eaton's Spring and Summer Catalogue
HTTPS://ARCHIVE.ORG/DETAILS/EATONS191600EATOUOFT

1917 Eaton's Spring and Summer Catalogue
HTTPS://ARCHIVE.ORG/DETAILS/EATONS191700EATOUOFT

1918 Sears Catalog by Sears, Roebuck and Company
HTTPS://ARCHIVE.ORG/DETAILS/CATALOG1918SEAR

1918 National Cloak & Suit Catalog, Private collection

1919-1920 New York styles : fall and winter by Perry, Dame & Co.
HTTPS://ARCHIVE.ORG/DETAILS/NEWYORKSTYLESFAL00PERR

1920 Spirella Catalog Private Collection

1920-21 Eaton's Fall and Winter Catalogue
HTTPS://ARCHIVE.ORG/DETAILS/EATONS19202100EATOUOFT

1921 Ferris Corset Catalog, Private Collection

1922 Charles Williams Catalog, Private Collection

1924 Spirella Instruction Book, Fifth Edition, Private Collection

www.ingramcontent.com/pod-product-compliance
Lightning Source LLC
Chambersburg PA
CBHW061152030426
42336CB00002B/20